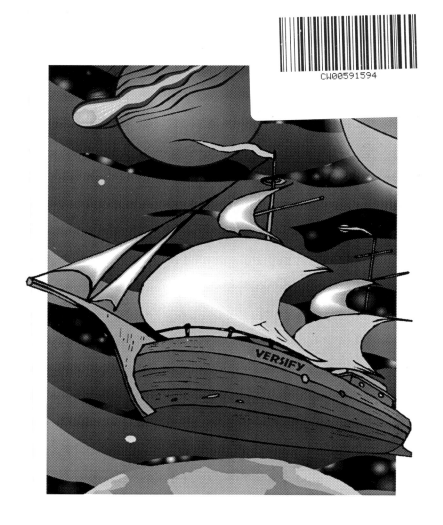

POETIC VOYAGES SOMERSET

Edited by Steve Twelvetree

CW00591594

First published in Great Britain in 2002 by
YOUNG WRITERS
Remus House,
Coltsfoot Drive,
Peterborough, PE2 9JX
Telephone (01733) 890066

All Rights Reserved

Copyright Contributors 2001

HB ISBN 0 75433 444 9
SB ISBN 0 75433 445 7

FOREWORD

Young Writers was established in 1991 with the aim to promote creative writing in children, to make reading and writing poetry fun.

This year once again, proved to be a tremendous success with over 88,000 entries received nationwide.

The Poetic Voyages competition has shown us the high standard of work and effort that children are capable of today. It is a reflection of the teaching skills in schools, the enthusiasm and creativity they have injected into their pupils shines clearly within this anthology.

The task of selecting poems was therefore a difficult one but nevertheless, an enjoyable experience. We hope you are as pleased with the final selection in *Poetic Voyages Somerset* as we are.

CONTENTS

Stephen Attwood	73
Bradley Baxter	73
Frances Foyne	74
Jordan Chambers	74
Alex Tallon	75
Carl Cawley	76
Rebecca Elliott	76
Chloe Burton	77
Sam Almond	77
Carla Tate	78
Kieren Moncur	79
Thomas May	79
Cassie Brown	80
James Plowman	80

North Newton CP School

Chloe Parchment	80
Gemma Hogg	81
Arran Watkins	82
Thomas Cottey	82
Sophie Carney	83
Charlotte Foster	84
Shaun Cook	84
Maria Perry	85
Rosie Anholt	85
Jake Burroughs	86
Rebecca Coram	86

North Petherton Junior School

Bethany Cude	87
Joseph Ellis	87
Bethan Langridge	87
Beau Ingram	88
Jack Curtis	88
Alice Michieli	88
James Fox	89
Matthew Warne	89
Kelly Parker	89

Amy Duddridge	90
Andrew Clark	90
Jessica Webber	90
Laura Baker	91

St Aldhelm's CE Primary School, Shepton Mallet

Bethany Manders	91
Louisa Garbett	92
Gemma Carver	92
Zoë Barnes	93
Esme Stevens	93
Nicola Pillinger	94
Ben Neale	94
Charlotte Mair	95
Samantha Fry	95
Vincent Wood Johnson	96
Alex Duchezeau	96
Lily Haggart	97
Suzy Corner	97
Fiona Stevens	98
Thomas Patterson	98
Jessica Wilkins	98
Robert Trick	99
Stephanie Walters	100

St John's RC School, Bath

Joel Pope	100
Theo Brand	100
Eilis Barrett	101
Rowland Goodbody	101
Bella Emery	102
Bethan Gray	102
James Indoe	102
Demelza Watkins	103
Thomas Southcott	103
Thomas Prangley	103
Hazel Walker	104
Brenden King	104

St Mary's Primary School, Bridgewater

St Paul's School, Shepton Mallet

Sedgemoor Manor Junior School

The Poems

TIME

If you look up into the sky,
You might see time fly quickly by.
For brown, orange, beige and gold,
Are the only colours time can hold.

Behind the sunset,
Clouds are near,
In the morning rise,
That seems so near.

Quickly darting from side to side,
Here comes time in the midnight sky.
Watch him swerve,
Watch him swish,
And disappear into the midnight mist.

Tara Hosking (10)
Abbas & Templecombe Primary School

THE PET

I don't know how you keep your fur so soft
I like to stroke your fur so nice
Generally I think it's magic
So how do you feel so soft?
That's right you're my pet.

All the fun you have
All the mice come in the house.
You get rid of them by tact.
That's right, you're my cat.

Edward Dyer (9)
Abbas & Templecombe Primary School

HOME

Home sweet home
Sweet home sweet.
I love my home.
Home!
Home!
I come home from school every day!
It's my best place!
It's
H
o
m
e.

Whenever I go outside
I've got my house to go
Home!
to.
Home sweet home.
Sweet home sweet.
I love my . . .
Home!

Ashlie Brabon (9)
Abbas & Templecombe Primary School

SNAKE

I see a snake
He's sliding through the long
Thick grass
He's always the last
But first he goes fast.

Vicky Cooper (8)
Abbas & Templecombe Primary School

ANIMALS

H orses are cute,
O ften they kick,
R unning around and
S oaring across the field
E ating grass and hay too.

D ogs are cuddly,
O thers are too,
G urgling water down their chin.

T igers are stripy,
I am not.
G oing to eat,
E at their food
R unning over grass hills.

P arrots are loud,
A nd very funny.
R ather not like other birds,
R ude talk all the time,
O ften though they didn't cross the line,
T he parrot is the funniest bird.

Kayleigh Cluett (9)
Abbas & Templecombe Primary School

YOUR TEACHER

Your teacher shouts
Your teacher laughs
Your teacher screams
Your teacher cries
Your teacher smokes
Your teacher runs.

Sam Benjafield (9)
Abbas & Templecombe Primary School

AT SCHOOL

Up and down the corridors,
In and out the classroom doors.
Up and up the stairs so high
Like an aeroplane in the sky!

We are all eating our lunch
The food in our mouths go munch, munch, munch.
We are all playing pick up sticks
The teachers think we're really thick!

We are playing games in the hall
We are playing with a big round ball.
When the bell rings, it's time for play
The teachers and children shout hip hip hooray!

Jack Sherry (10)
Abbas & Templecombe Primary School

ANIMALS

Cats all sit on my mats
Cats, cats, cats, and more cats.
Cats are in my hats
Cats, cats, cats and more cats.

Dogs are always on my logs
Dogs, dogs, dogs, and more dogs
Dogs are everywhere I go
Dogs, dogs, dogs and more dogs.

Rabbits are all in my cabinets
Rabbits, rabbits, rabbits and more rabbits
Rabbits are everywhere I go
Rabbits, rabbits, rabbits and even more rabbits.

Katherine Stone (10)
Abbas & Templecombe Primary School

WHEN I WALK IN THROUGH THE DOOR

When I walk in through the door
I can see my two cats, my dog and bird.
Bob Bob's in his box,
Bear Bear on the chair.
Gemma in a rage,
And Charlie in his cage.
When I walk in through the door,
I can hear the TV blasting.
You turn the channel and you can see,
People paper fastening.
When I walk in through the door
I can smell the tea burning.
Going through the kitchen door,
Whilst my dad is on the floor.
When I walk in through the door
I can feel the soft, gentle carpet,
Beneath my cold, frozen feet.
I sit on the blanket neat,
Putting my slippers on my feet.

Laura Smith (10)
Abbas & Templecombe Primary School

MY JOURNEY

Round the corner down the valley
Take a right and meet me in the alley.

This is the journey I had to take
To get someone a birthday cake.
It was big and round and blue
This special cake was for
        You!

Nick Thompson (10)
Abbas & Templecombe Primary School

MY KITTEN

My little kitten,
has got a pair of mittens.

He likes to play and fight,
and bounce all night.

My little kitten has got nice soft fur,
and he also likes to purr, purr, purr.

He's got big brown eyes,
And does small sighs.

My little kitten is big and strong,
but always does everything wrong.

That's why I love my little kitten.

Kayleigh Light (10)
Abbas & Templecombe Primary School

THE PLANETS

E   arth our home planet
A   great place to live
R   eally fun
T   he people are nice
H   ere at home.

M   ars so mysterious planet
A   n explorer's dream
R   eally weird
S   ome of Mars is uncovered.

S   un is the biggest planet
U   p high in the sky
N   early the greatest planet.

Tom Burt (11)
Abbas & Templecombe Primary School

MY GIRAFFE

My giraffe is big, my giraffe is tall,
My giraffe is not skinny or small.

He's got a very long neck,
And a sister called Beck.

My giraffe is orange, my giraffe is yellow,
He's a very, very, very fine fellow.

My giraffe has a brother called Fred
And a bed full of straw in a shed.

He eats lots of leaves
From the top of the trees.

And that's why I like my giraffe!

Harriet Moore (9)
Abbas & Templecombe Primary School

MY TEDDY BEAR

I've got a teddy bear, with a bow tie,
He's small and brown and likes to lie.

I've got a teddy bear, with a top hat,
He's big and black and got a friend called Rat.

I've got a teddy bear, in the bathroom,
He sits by the toilet loo.

I've got a teddy bear, who likes to laugh,
He sometimes sits in the playhouse.

I've got a teddy bear, who's really nice,
He's got eighty odd pet mice.

Charlotte England (9)
Abbas & Templecombe Primary School

CATS AND DOGS

Cats are like furry mats,
Except you can't stand on them.
Dogs are like big logs
Lying down all day.
Cats and dogs.

Cats are like little rats,
Running around all day.
Dogs are like bullfrogs
With wet noses.
Cats and dogs.

Cats are like tiny bats,
Swooping around at night.
Dogs are like ginormous hogs,
Always rolling in mud.
Cats and dogs.

Laura Cawley (10)
Abbas & Templecombe Primary School

GARBAGE DOG

He lives on a garbage tip
His nose can smell garbage from a mile away
He has a nasty nip
He has a kennel in the muck
He's much skinnier than a log
He has five spikes on the back of his head
He's a garbage dog.

Charlie Curran (9)
Abbas & Templecombe Primary School

MISTY DAYS!

Every new morning
I watch the sun and play
I try to be as good as gold
In every perfect way.

Every new morning
I wait beneath the clouds,
In misty or windy days,
I will try and be so *loud!*

Every new morning
I watch out my window,
To see good or bad,
Even evil or so sad.

So every new morning,
You fall asleep all day!

Sophie Penny (9)
Abbas & Templecombe Primary School

FARM LIFE

It has lots of cows.
It has pigs.
It has some chickens.
It has some sheep.
It makes me feel smelly.
Some of your meat comes from here.
You might get eggs from here.
You could die here.
It has lots of land here.
People come to collect milk from here.
It has machinery.

Tom Hunt (10)
Abbas & Templecombe Primary School

CROCODILE

If you ever go down to the Nile
If you see a green floating log
Don't take any notice.
Just please run away.
When it opens its mouth out wide,
That nice wide welcoming smile,
With hundreds of gleaming white sharp teeth,
It's bound to mean dinner is on its way
Snap
That nice welcoming smile snaps down
On some poor fish.
Don't let it be you, oh *please don't!*

Aidan Carolan (10)
Abbas & Templecombe Primary School

SCHOOL TIMES

Down and up the corridors
There we go on the floors
Ringing bells like wishing wells
Up and down the corridors.

When we go to look
You sometimes hear a crunch.
Up and down the corridors
La, la, la, la, la.

Everybody goes home from school
And says what a lovely day at school.

Verity Hamblin (10)
Abbas & Templecombe Primary School

ANIMALS

Elephants are big,
Giraffes are tall
Hippopotamuses are fat,
Mice are small.

Lizards are scaly,
Cats are soft
Fish and whales are slimy
And luckily they don't cough.

Crocodiles snap,
Dogs like to lick
Dolphins flip,
Horses kick.

Serena Guy (9)
Abbas & Templecombe Primary School

WALK WALK

Walk walk
Fast slow
Slow fast
Walk walk
Past people
In a hurry
Walk walk
Tall buildings
With busy people in.

Morgan Cartwright (9)
Abbas & Templecombe Primary School

BEST FRIENDS

Me and my friend go to the park together.
Swimming together, riding together
And everything together.

When we are in the park together,
We swing up and down on the see-saw,
Whiz down the slide and have lots of fun.

At swimming we splash around
And dunk each other in.

At riding school we have so much fun,
The horses dance and prance all the time.

Me and my friend go to the park together,
Swimming together, riding together,
And everything together.

Emma Talbot (11)
Abbas & Templecombe Primary School

TIGER

It moves stealthily and silently
Very fast and very clever
Camouflaged with grass,
It's very skilful.
It scares most animals,
Drinks water and eats meat.
Furry coat,
Moves on its own and not in packs,
It's a wild cat.

William Foers (9)
Abbas & Templecombe Primary School

SPRINGTIME

It couldn't be better
Just to send a letter
All about springtime.

When there's sudden showers,
And birds are singing,
And winters bring
Springtime.

Newborn babies
Only from the ladies
People getting ready for the spring.

Now I must go
Now I'm feeling low
But never mind
It's springtime.

Stephanie Kiddle (10)
Abbas & Templecombe Primary School

DINOSAURS

Dinosaurs are big
Dinosaurs are small
Dinosaurs are thick
Dinosaurs stink
Dinosaurs kill
Dinosaurs die
Dinosaurs are grim
But they are not slim.

Aaron Green (10)
Abbas & Templecombe Primary School

SPAIN

The palm trees were blowing in the breeze
You could hear the excitement from the people on the beach.
The colours were bright and cheerful
You could see the big boats in the distance
And the people on the pedaloes.
If you look you could only see a big blue sky
You could feel the heat of the beach.

Sean Mills (9)
Abbas & Templecombe Primary School

LOST IN THE WOODS

I could see trees, grass, birds
The colours were bright orange, brown, dark green.
There were some mountains in the distance
Then I saw a lion, I ran I was frightened
I ran into a big tree and then the lion sat on me.
Then I saw a human, he got me back home.

Kyle Ellis (8)
Abbas & Templecombe Primary School

I LOVE WRITING

I love writing I find it exciting
I could write about a beautiful princess
Or a girl in a pink frilly dress.
When I write, fireworks go off in my head.
When I write it makes me feel good,
Because I love writing and I find it exciting.

Amber Gray (8)
Abbas & Templecombe Primary School

TV

I like TV because I watch it every day
It's got my best programmes on
It's sometimes quiet, it's sometimes loud
I like Kenan & Kel because they're funny
I like Robot Wars because they battle
I like TV because I watch it everyday.

Matthew Biddiscombe (9)
Abbas & Templecombe Primary School

CHRISTMAS

It's Christmas night
There are owls hooting
There are fires glowing
Keeping people warm
And when people are asleep
Santa comes
Then in the morning
Everybody is excited.

William Foster (8)
Burrowbridge CE Primary School

MMMMMMM MILKY WAY

Gliding through the galaxy there's the Milky Way
Oh let me out I want to eat it mmmmmm.
I'm never talking to you again.
So that's my story of space.

Zak Bond (8)
Burrowbridge CE Primary School

WHEN YOUR IMAGINATION STARTS

When your imagination starts
Anything can happen,
Like ships floating in the sky
And even snakes in your bed.
When your imagination starts
Anything can happen.
Like a mouse attacking a cat
Or the sky in a pie.
A bird in a book
But when you look he's a cook
But
When your imagination starts
Nothing
Can stop it.

Yavanna Deadman (9)
Burrowbridge CE Primary School

COWBOYS

The cowboys lasso wild horses and bulls.
They catch fish.
They shoot ducks.
Cook them on the camp fire and
Eat them for tea.
After tea they sing songs and
Dance around the camp fire.
They make their tents with animal skin,
And wash in the streams every day.
That makes them say *Yee Haa*
Then they break camp and have another voyage.

Gary Hunt (9)
Burrowbridge CE Primary School

MY FERRETS

My ferrets eat turkey, ham and chicken.
They are lucky.
They play in their cage.
Dad, Jimmy and me take them rabbiting,
Digging and jumping in the water.
They like that.
I take them for walks on a lead.
I like my big, cuddly ferrets.

Gemma Collard (10)
Burrowbridge CE Primary School

CHRISTMAS

It's Christmas time again.
It's the night before Christmas.
And Father Christmas is coming.
He goes around about a hundred houses,
Before his work is done.
When he gets home he goes straight back to bed.
In February he starts all over again.

Gary Hard (10)
Burrowbridge CE Primary School

OCTOBER

In October I'll be a host to witches, goblins and ghosts.
I'll serve them turkey soup and rotting bread.
Whoopy once, whoopy twice
Whoopy turkey soup and rice.

Kirsty Fraser (7)
Burrowbridge CE Primary School

SPICE

Her shoes and her nails are like metal.
And when she walks it sounds like tick-tock.
Spice's body is a creamy colour
And her mane is like black and her tail is black.
The feed you have to put different stuff in there.
And if she's ill you have to give her special stuff.
Her blue eyes are beautiful and in the dark her eyes light up.
When she goes to a horse show
She gets excited.
Then afterwards we tack her up.
Then we get ready to jump
And when they call her name
She goes in the ring
With her voice she says
'Can I have some grub?'
Then she goes to bed.

Georgina Hurd (9)
Burrowbridge CE Primary School

THE SPELL OF THE WITCH

Goblins go witches dead
I'll cast a spell
Over your head.
Your light is round you look at the ground
Goblins go witches dead
I'll cast a spell
Over your head
And you will be dead.

Mikala Deadman (9)
Burrowbridge CE Primary School

THE OLD SPACE MAN

Once in the past there was an old man
He was one hundred and twenty six years old.
He is dead now.
He died going up into space.
It was a bit stupid going up into space at his age.
But he really wanted to, so they let him.
But the problem was he was very clumsy.
He kicked a pipe so he plastered it.
The next day he tipped some water on the pipe
So the plaster started to unpeel and all the gas leaked out.
The next day was his 126th birthday
So for a birthday treat he wanted a fag.
He got the lighter and when he lit the fag
The gas caught light and he and his spaceship blew up.

David Hawkins (10)
Burrowbridge CE Primary School

THE PICTURES

First you have to pay
By the counter.
Then you order your drinks and popcorn.
Cold and fizzy, crunchy.
Then you go in and sit down.
Soft and spongy.
Wait a minute, adverts come on before the show.
And it's dark and they do have curtains.
The audience are quiet.
And there is some music.
I was happy and I went to sleep at the end.
It was hot and dark.

Ian Foster (11)
Burrowbridge CE Primary School

LION

The small orange slinking thing stalking its prey.
Crawling along the ground getting closer and closer.
It breaks into a run and leaps.
The prey runs and so does the lion.
For that was what it was.
It leaps again and catches the game,
The lion will feast tonight.

James Barnes (11)
Burrowbridge CE Primary School

I WISH I WISH

I wish my journey wasn't so scary,
I wish my journey wasn't so bad,
I wish my journey wasn't so creepy,
I wish my journey wasn't so sad.

I wish my bus driver would let me go out,
I wish my bus driver wasn't so rude.
I wish my bus driver would let me creep about,
I wish my bus driver wasn't in such a bad mood.

I wish the people wouldn't be so noisy,
I wish the people wouldn't shout,
I wish the people wouldn't call me names
I wish the people wouldn't melt.

I wish the school bus was neat,
I wish the school bus wasn't so wonky,
I wish the school bus was tidy,
I wish the school bus wasn't so mouldy.

Charlotte Ham (8)
Horsington CE Primary School

MY OWN LITTLE PONY

I'm riding my own little pony
In a lovely green field,
I'm riding my own little pony
I feel I'm falling off.

I'm riding my own little pony
In a lovely green field,
With a whoosh of his tail
And a swish of his head
I travel on to the field ahead.

I'm riding my own little pony
In a lovely green field.
I'm galloping over the jumps,
I'm going down with a *Thump!*

Sophie Jamieson (9)
Horsington CE Primary School

GIANT BUGS

Giant ants come from Mars
And land on Earth
No one can escape the
Big red creatures.

Two years later a giant spider
Arrived on Earth
Destroying the ants
And then destroying the world.

He goes back to space
And there is a surprise attack by Martians.

Tom Lees (8)
Horsington CE Primary School

SEA THINGS

S ee the seahorses swim in the sea.
E lectric eels are electric
    Don't touch them or they'll electrocute me.
A fraid of baby octopuses, *not me*
T he dolphins are appealing I agree.
H I Flipper balance a ball on your nose for me.
I wish to stay here all day and night.
N ear water and creatures
G o creatures and be free
S wim near and far, go here and there
    Creatures are *everywhere.*

Lucy Sanger (8)
Horsington CE Primary School

A HAIR BAND

I'm looking for a hair band
A where band? A hair band
To tie my hair back with a hair band.
And have some fun.
To tie my long hair back
And have some more fun.
And run outdoors with the dogs
Stretching stretching
Torture!

Amelia Rowland (8)
Horsington CE Primary School

COME ON BUS DRIVER

Come on bus driver, go faster,
You're going as slow as a snail.
An ant would go faster than you.
Bus driver someone needs the loo.

Bus driver I need to get to school
Today not sometime next year.
Probably the same with all the other people,
Ha you made it to school.

Luke White (8)
Horsington CE Primary School

I SWIM

I swim over the Antarctic,
It is extremely cold.
I swim over the sky,
And I fall in a cloud.

I swim over the Indian Ocean
And then there is a windy storm
I swim over all the oceans
And it was really great fun.

I swim in my hotel pool,
Then I dive straight in,
I swim in the sea,
It is so warm.

Imogen Clayton (7)
Horsington CE Primary School

MARS

Moving through the sky
Astronauts are coming
Rattling through the air
Sheltering through the soft breeze.

Stephanie Crofts (7)
Horsington CE Primary School

ON THE BUS

I'm going on a trip
I'm going on a trip
Oh no this seat is hard and lumpy.

I'm going on a trip
I'm going on a trip
Oh no this bus is slow and bumpy.

I'm going on a trip
I'm going on a trip
Oh hooray, we've arrived
I'm getting off the bus
Bumpy humpy stumpy
Clumpy ride.

Ryan White (7)
Horsington CE Primary School

SPACE

I'm ready to lift off
After five my jets come on
I'm off to the moon
At a fast fast speed.
My jets are rumbling
Watch me go past the stars,
Jupiter and Mars.
We are reaching the moon
Now I am landing.
My passengers get their suits on
Ka-Boom I'm off back to land.

Sam Shead (8)
Horsington CE Primary School

UNDER THE SEA WORLD

Under the sea fish, sea horses, crabs
Wander about the coral.

Under the sea sharks peep round rocks.

Under the sea, seaweed swirls and
Dolphins play.

Under the sea, clownfish dance
Shells open and clack.

Under the sea I dance with the animals.

Under the sea I swim with mermaids.

Rachael Fox (7)
Horsington CE Primary School

UNDER THE SEA

I dive under the water
I see a sea horse turning gracefully
I see a fish in a net under the sea.

What a beautiful world under the sea.
I see seaweed dancing under the sea.
Look at that shark hiding behind a rock.

What a beautiful sight it is under the sea
Sea monkeys under the sea.

I wish I lived under the sea.
What a beautiful sight it can be.

Tom Rumbelow (7)
Horsington CE Primary School

THE SEA DRAGON

One stormy night
In winter by the sea
The waves were rough
And I couldn't believe
What was happening to me.

I was being carried away by a sea dragon
With fluffy fur
I still couldn't believe what was happening to me
I thought it would never occur.

And nothing happened for a while,
The dragon was taking me under the sea.
I couldn't believe what the coral seaweed was doing,
It was dancing, I still couldn't believe what was
                              happening to me.

Polly Hancock (7)
Horsington CE Primary School

THE ORANGE PEEL

The orange peel falling down and down
Into the bin.
Falling through the air
Down and down it goes
Into the smelly bin.

Falling and falling
Like a pin
Eventually coming to the edge of the bin
Down it goes into the smelly bin.

Charlotte Bristow (7)
Horsington CE Primary School

TRAVELLING FISH

Fish travelling through the rough sea,
Thrown about by the crashing waves,
Loads of ships have crashed on rocks,
Bits of wood are everywhere.

Fish travelling through the calm river
Slowly swimming along between the stones,
Quite a sight for human eyes,
As they travel upstream.

Fish travelling through the wild ocean,
Narrowly missing a shark's mouth,
Scared and frightened they are,
As they journey on their way.

Lizzie Antell (8)
Horsington CE Primary School

MY VOYAGE TO DARTMOUTH

Misty windows,
Boiling hot.
Squashed up luggage right to the top,
Yummy sweets should do the trick,
Now I'm starting to feel sick.

Mummy's car is old and blue,
Fat and chubby and stinky too.
Twisty roads and pouring rain,
I wish I was back home again.

Annabel Stanford (7)
Horsington CE Primary School

A SPACESHIP JUST FOR ME

I'm making my own little spaceship,
Out of a dustbin can.
I'm working very hard on it,
Using paper, nails and tools.

Mum comes out with a big red face,
'What's the matter Mum?' I asked.
She told me 'what's the matter?'
And I say 'Oh no not again.'

I clear up all the mess on the floor,
'That's better James,'
Then secretly,
I do it all again!

I try to get in my spaceship,
But it doesn't go.
I'll never make it into space,
Oh no, oh no, oh no!

Amber Allinson-Epps (9)
Horsington CE Primary School

I'M LOOKING FOR A . . .

I'm looking for a train station
I'm looking for a train
I'm looking for a carriage
I'm looking for a comfy seat
I'm looking for a way out
I'm looking for a step
I'm looking for a passenger
I'm looking for a cushion.
I finally found my way out of the train.

Joshua Farrant (8)
Horsington CE Primary School

THE FLYING SCHOOL BUS

A school bus,
With wings parked in the playground
It was bright yellow
Its wings were silvery white.

It was as fast as a plane,
and as big as a classroom.
The children got on
as it started up.

The bus zoomed round
And its wings flapped
Faster and faster,
Then it took off.

The bus zoomed round
and round it went.
Past the clouds, past the moon
past Mars, past Venus and stopped.

The driver got out
And floated to the front
Poured in petrol
Got back and in turned the bus round.

They went past Venus
Past Mars, past the moon.
Past the clouds and back to Earth
The children said 'That was fun.'

Paul Durant (7)
Horsington CE Primary School

PEACH

I wish I had a peach,
I wish I could go to space in it.
I wish I could see the sun,
I wish it was all done.

I wish I could float on air,
I wish I could see all the planets,
I wish I could see the moon men,
I wish I could always play with them.

I wish I could go to Pluto, no Mars,
I wish I could touch the sun,
I wish it was not too hot,
I wish I had a lot.

Alice Maltin (8)
Horsington CE Primary School

THE WORLD

The world is an enormous face
Spain is the nose
England is the eyeball
Scotland is the other eyeball
The sea is the world's tears.

The world is a washing machine
Big and round, it goes around
And around like the world.
They are both strong.
It's very wrong
And weird for a washing machine
To be as useful as the world.

Joseph Phippard (8)
Hutton CE VC Primary School

CLASS 4

Class 4 is a big class,
There's 33 in all,
And everybody in this class,
Drives Mrs Champ up the wall.

She teaches English, maths and history,
And art we like the best,
But not very many like
The very hard maths test.

Now Henry VIII had six wives,
And one of them survived,
But some of them were unlucky,
And quite quickly died.

Now these are things you ought to know,
Otherwise go back to school,
And learn about English, maths and history,
And art, we think is cool.

Katie Hutchings (8)
Hutton CE VC Primary School

THE STORM

Rain pouring in the morning,
Lightning clashing, thunder crashing.
Forks of lightning lighting up the sky,
Like people up there waving goodbye.
Rain pouring in the morning,
Lightning clashing, thunder crashing.

Hailstones pattering on the window outside,
Watching two thunderstorms collide.

Joe Brady (8)
Hutton CE VC Primary School

THE SKY

The sky is a patchwork quilt . . .
Birds are in the patchwork sky,
Watching sewn aeroplanes fly by.
Each bird has a detailed beak,
But each one is unique.
The sun is made of delicate thread,
All glowing warmly golden red.
The clouds are made of fine silk,
Each one the colour of milk.
At night are the silver threaded stars,
And also the planets like Jupiter and Mars.
There are spaceships and a satellite,
And comets that shine so bright.
All in the patchwork sky!

Amy Hutson (9)
Hutton CE VC Primary School

THUNDERSTORM

Thunder clashing
Lightning flashing
Lightning bashing
Thunder rumbling
Trees tumbling.
Forks of lightning shooting
Jolting blades of lightning
Lightning clashing and crashing
Thunder rumbling, clambering,
Dogs barking.
Thunder makes strange noises.

Tim Page (8)
Hutton CE VC Primary School

THE WASHING MACHINE

The water is washing,
The dirty clothes faster and faster
And making it zoom and whiz.

It is magic; the washing machine is spinning fast and slow,
Making powder bubbles rise around the room.

The whizzing clothes are finally washed,
It is slowing down, slow, slow, and in the end
It finally stops . . .

And all the bubbles all die down and all
Go . . .
Pop

Laura Clarkson (8)
Hutton CE VC Primary School

THE THUNDERSTORM

Clashing, dashing, screaming,
The lightning is brightening the sky,
Bashing, booming,
It blinds my right eye,
Whooshing, sparkling, noisy,
The dangerous lightning drops are like rain,
Frightening, zooming, exciting,
Banging on the edge of my brain,
Flashing, clanging, shocking,
The thunderstorm rose last night,
Dangerous, screaming, banging,
It gave me a great big fright,
Whoosh!

Stacey Howell (9)
Hutton CE VC Primary School

HOMEWORK

Homework is so boring
Sometimes I start snoring.

Mum shouts 'Get on with it,'
I start to feel like I've fallen in a pit.

I start to write my 'look, cover, write, check,'
Then on the paper I see a speck.

My mum shouts 'Tea',
So I say, 'A break, yes, yippee.'

My mum says 'How's the homework coming?'
My dad says, 'Did you use words that are stunning?'

I've finished my tea,
Oh no, crikey.

I hope I'll get a merit
and the extra credit.

Rheanna Carter (8)
Hutton CE VC Primary School

THE ALIENS ARE HERE

The aliens are here and it's time to go.
The aliens are also green.
If you go near them, it will be painful
And give you a scare.

They have green arms and big black eyes
That's what the aliens are like.

Richard Cooksley (8)
Hutton CE VC Primary School

WINTER

It's freezing outside, I'm very cold
My grandma says she's very old
She will miss the fun and games
We will have to introduce their names.

It's freezing outside, I'm very cold
The snow is melting brightly gold
It was snowing all night
I looked out, what a lovely sight.

It's cold outside, I'm freezing
And my mum's sneezing
But I can't go out to play.

Rebecca Alford (9)
Hutton CE VC Primary School

THE ALIENS

The UFO is full of baby trees,
They have splinters on their knees.
They're gruesome,
They're scary.

They're toosum
And hairy.
They have big warts,
And polka dot shorts.
They have tall hats
And very hairy cats.
They are the aliens.

Adam Berry (8)
Hutton CE VC Primary School

FOOD

First, in the morning
I sometimes have toast,
I like it with butter
But jam I like the most.

On Sundays we have a roast
With carrots and chicken too.
When my mum says we're having a roast
I shout yabba dabba doo.

For tea we have fish and chips
With salt and vinegar on top
If we buy it really fresh
It's always way too hot.

For pudding I usually have sweets
And sometimes chocolate ice cream.
If I have both of these
My eyes will start to gleam.

When I eat all of this
My teeth start to hurt
Then something else comes next,
Pop, diddle, burp.

Amie Johnston (8)
Hutton CE VC Primary School

WINTER

I looked outside to see the sparkling snow
Then looked at the trees, at the leaves that would not grow.
It's freezing in the night,
When it's windy, I fly my kite.

The winter seems like it never ends,
It's so cold outside I can't play with my friends.
It's not like the summer breeze,
It's hard, cold wind, I'll probably freeze.

Ann-Marie Geer (8)
Hutton CE VC Primary School

THE DARK

The dark is like a big, black star across the sky,
The dark is like being locked in a cupboard,
It makes me feel scared.

The dark is like hiding under your bed,
The dark is like being lost in a coal mine,
It makes me feel scared.

The dark is like being in a tomb,
The dark is like being in a cave,
It makes me feel scared.

The dark is all gloomy,
The dark is like being lost in space,
It makes me feel scared.

The dark is like a cellar,
The dark is like a big, black cloud across the sky,
It makes me feel scared.

The dark is like a big dark room,
The dark is like a big chocolate bar,
It makes me feel scared.

Alice Withers (9)
Hutton CE VC Primary School

GHOSTS

Look out, look out,
Ghosts are about,
Get in the house,
And don't come out.
In the bedroom,
They are there so,
Beware, beware, beware.

They are there on the stair,
Up and down, beware, beware,
Move around the house at night,
And you will get quite a fright.

If you close your eyes,
At night, bye-bye to you
That's alright,
You say that's not fair,
Beware, beware, beware.

Amy Taylor (9)
Hutton CE VC Primary School

THE MONSTER

The monster is big and hairy and scary,
His scales are as big as a leaf,
And his tail is like roast beef.
He storms around like an elephant.
In bed his tail goes mad,
And he gets back up again from
Falling down,
And then he storms to his bed,
That is as big as a lake.

Charlotte Dyer (8)
Hutton CE VC Primary School

FALLING DOWNSTAIRS

As I was falling down the stairs
It is so scary falling down the stairs.
There's lots of blood.

Going in the ambulance
Going through the traffic
With light flashing in my eyes.

Going into the X-ray room
With light flashing in my eyes
Not getting put to sleep.

After seven days my stitches come out
Now I've just got a scar.
I feel like a *star*.

Brodie McLeish (9)
Hutton CE VC Primary School

MONSTERS

Monsters are colossal
and they eat fossils.

Monsters are scary
and they are hairy.

Monsters lick blood
and go thud, thud.

Peter Ratcliffe (8)
Hutton CE VC Primary School

WINTER

Winter is as cold as ice
You need to wrap up warm
Because if you go outside today
You're sure to need coats on.

At winter everything is dead
You're sure to see no colour
Especially crimson red.

Sometimes at winter it begins to snow
So you'd better get your sledges out
Before the crisp snow melts.

Rachel Jones (8)
Hutton CE VC Primary School

WINTER

It's cold outside and I'm freezing,
My mum's shivering,
My dad's quivering.

It's cold outside and I'm sneezing,
It's snowing and our
Evergreen plants are showing.

It's cold outside and it's very icy,
My mum says let's go indoors,
My dad says he'll make mince pies.

Helen Pound (8)
Hutton CE VC Primary School

MONSTERS

Monsters are hairy and scary,
They have huge tails to rip up mail.

Monsters are gigantic, sometimes they are
Mechanic,
At night, they look a terrible sight.

His mean, green eyes shine at you,
I think he wants to eat you, me too.

He has an electric tail if he gets you
You will make a wail.

He spies at you with mean, green eyes.

Daniel Liddiard (8)
Hutton CE VC Primary School

WINTER'S BACK

It was snowing all through the chilly night,
And when I woke up I saw a lovely sight.

I started to play in the wonderful snow,
And when I went to bed
The sparkly snow started to glow.

The very next day there was a lot of breeze,
And in the afternoon I started to freeze.

Jennifer Harrison (8)
Hutton CE VC Primary School

THE MONSTER

The monster is a deadly beast.

I am huge and scary
I am bloodcurdling
Beware, beware, beware,
I am spotty with a huge tail and it
Is spiky.

James Orchard (9)
Hutton CE VC Primary School

THE DARK

The dark has sometimes lightning
But always it is frightening.
It is really spooky; only
In the dark
The stars shine and
The moon makes really cool
Shadows.

Ben Stamp (9)
Hutton CE VC Primary School

THE MOON

The moon is bright and powerful.
The moon is so strong, the mysterious
glowing beam goes on, on and on.
The beam that I keep on seeing,
gets bright every night.

Sean Booth (8)
Hutton CE VC Primary School

THE DARK

I'm afraid of the dark
especially in the park.
Even my cousin Mark
is afraid of the dark, so
even me and my cousin
Mark is afraid of the dark.
So if you are in the dark do
not be afraid of the dark like
me and my cousin Mark.

Jessica Gaman (9)
Hutton CE VC Primary School

PANDA

Panda, panda trudging through the bamboo,
Anywhere she will go to find her long lost cub.
Never stopping to eat, never stopping to sleep,
But she's thinking,
'Dying, dying my darling could be dying.
Anything for her, just keep her alive.
Stop, look, here she is but . . . what? . . .
A terrible sight, a terrible sight.
Rolo, my baby, you're trapped in a deer trap.
Aliens, hunters, children and adults.
Put these here in our territory.
Poachers want our soft warm fur,
Elegance always goes the wrong way.
Dying she is, I must set her free.
Now I can do something that will help
Our youngest panda cub,
We can all now be free.
Her and me!'

Lorna Stace (10)
Keinton Mandeville Primary School

A TASTY MEAL

Hi! I'm called lettuce.
The sky is blue,
And it's nice to see you too.

Hi! I'm called caterpillar,
I'm green and I'm clean.
I like to eat juicy green lettuce.
Hang on! That's lettuce over there.
Yum! That tastes good.

Hi! I'm called bird.
I like to fly high in the sky.
I like to eat juicy green caterpillars,
Hang on! I spy with my little eye,
I think I see something beginning with 'c'.
Yes, that's right - a caterpillar.

Hi! I'm called cat,
And I am on a hunt for birds.
There's one! That didn't take very long to find.
Now then, all I have to do,
Is creep up as quietly as possible,
And then catch him.
Ready? Go! Yes, got him!
A bit bony but tastes good.

Lauren Gornall (10)
Keinton Mandeville Primary School

A SNOWDROP

Its fragile petals, timid and white,
Trying, trying to hold on tight.
Weaving its way to the top.
Wait right there and the bud may pop.

Glossy white and jungle green,
Its sweet smelling pollen only for the bees.
Slowly, slowly it will grow,
What will happen no one knows.

Lynsey Waterhouse (11)
Keinton Mandeville Primary School

THE GOLDEN EAGLE

He's gold like sunlight,
Soaring in the air,
He's proud of his wings,
Broad and strong.

His talons are like gold,
Irreplaceable.
He needs his talons for they are
Broad and strong.

His beak is powerful,
Like big machinery.
He likes his beak, it makes him look
Broad and strong.

His feathers are soft
But not for touching.
His feathers make him look,
Broad and strong.

As poachers arrive,
He's not aware they're looking for him.
Bang! The golden eagle is no longer
Broad and strong.

William Gledhill (11)
Keinton Mandeville Primary School

THE CHEETAH

On its private little mound
Watching, watching,
It stalks its prey without a sound,
Waiting, waiting.

Getting restless it moves in,
Slowly, slowly.
It knows that it can win,
Spying, spying.

It breaks into a run,
Faster, faster.
Taking its prey away from the group,
Fighting fighting.

It drags down the helpless victim,
Winning, winning.
And then the suffocating bite,
Killing, killing.

The predator drags back its dead victim,
Pulling, pulling.
Onto its little private mound,
Eating, eating.

The killer has won.

Charles Chinnock (11)
Keinton Mandeville Primary School

SPACE

Stars glowing in the dark,
Earth taking its time,
Moon doing its job,
Astronauts floating in space,
Spacecraft landing.

Astronauts walking,
Rockets shooting up,
Fire blasting down,
Colours blending in the planets,
Spacecraft lifting off.

Simon Hunter (11)
Keinton Mandeville Primary School

NO ONE IS SAFE

Isn't it nice and sunny today?
Sitting with my friends, having a play.
In the shady sugar packet,
Fairly safe from the daily racket.

Hey dudes, I'm Dan the fly,
Just licking sugar until I die.
Sugar really is so tasty,
Though I don't eat it too hasty.

What's that up by the sill?
Oh, it's a fly that's looking ill.
I'll swallow him up in one big slurp,
All I need now is one big burp.

Hi, my name's Paul the Pike,
'Ello there's my dinner, Yum, that's right.
Raw frog meat, Mmmm that's nice,
Tastes a bit like curry and rice.

Look! Bubbles in the stream,
Be quick - call for the fishing team.
Wahoo they've finally got the pike,
Though he put up a desperate fight.

David Brock (10)
Keinton Mandeville Primary School

WATCH OUT!

I'm such a pretty lettuce growing in the ground,
It is so quiet here, I can't hear a sound.
Oh, no! What do I see?
I think it is a caterpillar coming to eat me.

It will be such a lovely lunch,
I think I'll eat that lettuce, munch, munch, munch.
Oh no! What do I see?
I think it is a bird coming to eat me.

Look! A big, fat juicy caterpillar sitting on the soil.
What shall I do? Grill, fry or boil?
Oh no! What do I see?
I think it is a cat, coming to eat me.

Oooh . . . what a fine treat today,
I'll have to pluck the feathers, hooray, hooray.
Oh yes I am as safe as could be,
Because nothing at all can ever eat me!

Heidi Hellings (11)
Keinton Mandeville Primary School

THE RABBITS

It was a blowy night,
When two rabbits started to fight.
They were shivery and cold,
As the days go by, they're getting old.

Rabbits leaping to the sun,
Trying to have lots of fun.
Making the most of their days,
In many, many sorts of ways.

Two rabbits fighting over food,
Getting in a very bad mood,
Stuck in their cage day by day,
Having nothing, nothing to say.

Rabbits leaping to the sun,
Trying to have lots of fun,
Making the most of their days,
In many, many sorts of ways.

Samantha Edwards (11)
Keinton Mandeville Primary School

THE GUARD DOG

I'm stuck in a cage,
Beginning to age,
I want to run free,
Why can't it be?

He lets me out,
When no one's about,
Always at night, never at day,
All I want to do is jump up and play.

If anyone comes, they race off in a hurry,
They think I don't worry.
Sometimes at night,
They put up a fight.

The part I enjoy?
When they give me a toy.
I'm stuck in a cage,
Beginning to age.

William Upchurch (10)
Keinton Mandeville Primary School

SNOWDROPS

White like a swan, gentle and free,
Their nectar is sweet and charms a bee.
Soft and dainty with delicate petals,
Not a bit alarmed by any nettles.

Snowdrops spread near and far,
People pick them and put them in a jar.

They are like snowflakes, still upon the floor,
Lying outside a kitchen door,
Little tints of green glimmer through,
Each one looks as if brand new.

Snowdrops spread near and far,
People pick them and put them in a jar.

Lyndsay Putland (11)
Keinton Mandeville Primary School

A BRICK HOUSE

A brick house standing tall,
It will never fall,
It is old,
It is cold.

It has a stable,
With a table,
It is owned by Mick,
He has a mate called Nick.

A brick house standing tall,
It will never fall,
It is old,
It is cold.

Nicholas Hunter (11)
Keinton Mandeville Primary School

ZEBRA

I'm black and white,
Like a horse.
I'm fast and speedy,
Sometimes lost.

I'm in a group most of the time,
Eating grass, that's my aim.
Sometimes scared, mostly happy,
I will never ever stray from my pack party.

People like my stripy coat,
I like it but I don't like to boast,
Some people say I'm really absurd,
But I say I'm *OK* for a zebra!

Abby Baker (11)
Keinton Mandeville Primary School

THE CHIMPANZEE

Swinging from side to side,
Looking out, far and wide,
He's coming to the metal bars,
When night falls, he sees stars.

Swinging and swaying!

The stars are shining very bright,
They give him a little fright.
Showing off his new brown coat,
Nothing like a scruffy grey goat.

Swinging and swaying!

Zara Robinson (10)
Keinton Mandeville Primary School

VOICES

It was dark.
Voices I heard.
To me a mumble.

Light bewildered me.
I was scared,
My mouth screamed.
Faces surrounded me.

A silent face approached me,
A sweet smell,
A gentle voice sang as it calmed me,
A rocking motion within me.

The doors open,
I giggle.
The smell of polluted air drowns my laughter.
A hammering noise frustrates me.
My head is banging.
The buildings tower above me, looking down.

The doors open,
I giggle quietly,
A warm softness beneath my head,
Sweet music surrounds me,
My eyes are closing.
A drowsy feeling within me.

It was dark.

Hannah D'Ovidio (10)
Keinton Mandeville Primary School

REX THE RABBIT

His beautiful white coat like snowdrops,
Pink innocent eyes stare at you
As if you've done
Something wrong.

Rex, the rabbit.

His pink, innocent eyes stop staring,
They turn big and bold.
He hops round with happiness,
In his hutch.

Rex, the rabbit.

It's starting to rain and Rex is unhappy,
He looks as if he's crying.
But he still stands out in the rain,
Like a beam of light.

Rex, the rabbit.

It's time to feed him, but he's gone.
A puddle of blood,
And a pile of bones,
Lying there.

Rex, the rabbit.

Adam Miles (10)
Keinton Mandeville Primary School

THE CHEETAH

The cheetah starts to get hungry,
Searches and searches for prey.
Never stops looking,
There's food in sight,
Starts creeping,
Getting closer and closer . . .
Go! Go! Go!
Starts running swiftly like the wind,
Like a Ferrari speeding down the road.
He pounces and bounces.
He misses.
He starts again, lands right on top,
Bites round the neck,
Suffocating his food,
As his prey falls,
To the ground.

Jack Tucker (10)
Keinton Mandeville Primary School

THE CAMEL

He walks through the scorching hot desert,
Plodding slowly through the grainy sand,
Carrying a man and his load,
Further and further from his town,
Never giving up,
With his padded feet and his sharp black eyes,
Brave as anyone could be,
He walks through the desert.

Night falls and the man sleeps
While the camel plods on.
At last he lays down to rest.
The night goes by.
They start their journey again.
Hour after hour they plod on,
Until they reach their destination.

Louis Cross (11)
Keinton Mandeville Primary School

BABY TIGER CUB

Little black stripes,
Soft orange fur.
Little black nose,
Baby tiger cub.

Bright and bubbly,
Cute and bouncy,
Little wet paws,
Baby tiger cub.

Roaming the jungle,
Pouncing and prowling,
Stalking flies,
Baby tiger cub.

Little black stripes,
Soft orange fur,
Little black nose,
Baby tiger cub.

Katie Joyce (10)
Keinton Mandeville Primary School

BEAUTIFUL BUTTERFLY

Beautiful butterfly
Fluttering by,
Colours amazing
Spread on its wings.

Daintily dancing
And on flowers resting,
In among petals
It hovers above nettles.

Delicate, beautiful
Fragile and careful
It spreads its wings
While a gentle breeze sings.

Fluttering by,
The butterfly.

Elizabeth Teague (10)
Keinton Mandeville Primary School

THE SHARK

He makes his way,
Rippling the water silently.
His terrible teeth,
And his heavy skin.

He makes his way,
Through the windy seas,
He makes it easy,
With his heavy load.

He does his best,
In loneliness.
He collects his prey,
With his heavy, droopy mouth.

He smells his way,
Through the deep blue ocean,
Making his way,
With his heavy body.

Robert Lukins (10)
Keinton Mandeville Primary School

THE SNOWDROP

Green and delicate,
White and fragile.
Dainty and shy,
Skinny and scared.

Hoping not to get chosen,
Worshipping the sun,
Standing delicately,
Praying for warmth.

Beautiful and sweet,
Frail and wilted,
Family and friends nearby,
Comforting and reassuring.

Green and delicate,
White and fragile.

Chantel Ashby (10)
Keinton Mandeville Primary School

THE DOLPHIN

The dolphin swimming gracefully in the cool blue water,
Jumping out and performing acrobatics before diving back in,
Greeting any fishermen with a cheerful squeal.
Its sleek body cutting and shaping the water,
Catching small fish thanks to its excellent navigation,
It communicates with its friends with echo location.
So happy in its wonderful world of swimming and splashing.
Diving down to the murky coral and seaweed that lies forgotten
and shy,
The dolphin swimming gracefully in the cool blue water.

Carly Willmott (11)
Keinton Mandeville Primary School

THE SHARK

The shark swims through the coral reef,
Waiting for her prey.
She swims with a sleek and slow pace,
Until she sees something and dodges to the side.
Going after her prey, with mighty strength,
Then suddenly the whole sea goes a bloody red.

The shark swims through the coral reef,
With her beady eyes and her long thin body,
Her bony jaws hold her sharp and vicious teeth,
Her back fin splits the water as she swims,
She's so graceful, the predator of everything.

Vanessa Goodwin (11)
Keinton Mandeville Primary School

THE AEROPLANE FLIGHT

The aeroplanes were orange and yellow
They flew to Cyprus, America and France.
All those places are hot and sunny,
My journey is to Cyprus
It is my second time.
I dream of flying to my swimming pool
The biggest and deepest in the world.
On the back of the aeroplane seats are TV's.
I watched Titanic and James Bond.
I looked out of the window and saw the mountains.
They were rugged and gravelly.
I like views.
That's why I sit by the window
Flying is the best way to travel.

Sam Harding (9)
Monteclefe CE VA Junior School

THE HORSE'S JOURNEY

The horse was galloping very fast
Across the lake
And through the forest
Over the desert
And round the moor
Into his stable.
He runs out of it
Runs over the desert
And through the forest
Across the lake
Back to his home.

Scott Robbins
Monteclefe CE VA Junior School

BOAT

The boat was zooming through the water.
It is red and gold.
It went very slow.
The sun came up.
It has got very shiny.
It was beautiful.
It went 190 miles an hour,
Towards the finish line.
The boat has won the race.
Some fish got killed.
A great big blue came.
All of a sudden,
In a flash of light,
It was gone.
The boat sailed on,
Back to the shore.

Jack Wright (7)
Monteclefe CE VA Junior School

THE HORSE RIDE

Along the dusty roads
Through the trees we go
Feeling the long grass
Smelling the scented flowers.
The sun shines warmly on my back
Glowing red and yellow.
Climbing high in the morning
Through the misty meadow.

Edward Squire (9)
Monteclefe CE VA Junior School

THE RACE BEGINS

I travel through the sky
In my purple air balloon.
I pull a lever and release the fire
Which is orange, red and yellow.
I'm in a race
It's very hot and sunny.
I'm in the second place.
I feel very, very proud.
Down below me is a forest
Which looks like a great big cauliflower.
Zoom along.
And I am side by side
At the front.
I'm shaking and shivering,
But I pass the finishing line and I've won.
Everyone cheers and claps their hands,
As the man hands me his trophy.

Ruth Power (9)
Monteclefe CE VA Junior School

THE CROCODILE

The crocodile has dark slimy skin
And a bumpy back.
He has a long green, slithery tail
And nostrils as big as your toe.
He may bite you with a snap, snap
Of his big sharp teeth,
As he glides through the swamp.
He will gobble you up with a gulp.

Lauren Walker (9)
Monteclefe CE VA Junior School

THE RUNAWAY CAR

The car zooms along,
Going faster and faster.
As fast as it can.
Stop! Stop!
Catch the car.
I want the car.
The car is blue and red.
It is starting again.
It's going again
Faster and faster,
Down the hill,
Heading for a disaster.
At the bottom of the hill is a tree.
Bump.
It hits the tree.
It stops.

Tammy Farenden (7)
Monteclefe CE VA Junior School

THE JOURNEY IN THE FOREST

Heading to the living forest
Green and gloomy.
I don't like this
I have to find my black gorilla.
His eyes are like red traffic lights
Looking and looking,
I still can't find him.
Tree to tree branches to branches.
Going through the living forest
Gloomy dark and wet.

Michael Giles
Monteclefe CE VA Junior School

MY JOURNEY ON MANY THINGS

You can travel into space,
Or any little place.
Go by car,
And you can go far.
Go by plane,
And you can go to Spain.
Go by train and it's sure to rain.
Go by bus,
And you won't get in a fuss.
Be really cool and go to school,
On your scooter.

But most important, don't forget the things
On the end of your legs.
   Feet!

Kayleigh Bingham (9)
Monteclefe CE VA Junior School

MY CONVERTIBLE

Red, silver and gold
It zooms through the desert
With dusty doors and dusty wheels
Rockets rumble from within.
It has a boot
You could fit an elephant in
And a powerful, fast and smooth engine.
My convertible
Is king of the desert.

Richard Duffield (8)
Monteclefe CE VA Junior School

THE CAR

The smoky whoosh on the bumpy road,
Twisting and speeding along the road.
I knew it would be a long way,
Scratches and scars from a gun,
Petrol is what I need.
I can travel at
10
20
30
40
50
60 miles an hour.
I am red and blue.
At last I am there
In France, dusty and dirty.
Muddy, grubby.

Lance Gosden (7)
Monteclefe CE VA Junior School

MY HORSE

My horse is golden and brown.
She has diamond eyes.
She has a black shiny tail.
She gallops fast.
Faster than a lion,
Over the long straight course.
She jumps like the wind
And moves as gracefully as a swan
And is as beautiful as a rainbow.

Hannah Lock (7)
Monteclefe CE VA Junior School

SAILING A YACHT

Looking at the islands one by one
Seeing all the things that are going on.
Seagulls swooping down looking for a fish,
Look at the dolphins doing a back flip,
Swooping in the water
One by one so elegant.
The waves are crashing on the boat,
Swish, swash, swash.
My yacht is brown and golden,
It glints in the sun,
We are nearly there now,
But I'll be back again,
You bet I will.

Jessica McCreery (9)
Monteclefe CE VA Junior School

THE CHEETAH

Fast as a speeding bullet
Racing through the jungle,
And across the African plains
As the cheetah stalks its prey.
As hunters come for the cheetah's skin,
It travels at night
In the darkness
In the meadows,
Away from the danger.
He sprints at the sounds
Of the hunter's gun.
He escapes.

Karl Gardner (9)
Monteclefe CE VA Junior School

THE TRAIN

The big dark green steam train,
Waiting at the station in Somerton.
A jolly driver stepped into the train.
'All aboard' he called.
Everyone stepped onto the large train.
There were comfortable seats,
Small windows to look out of.
A lovely view to see.
The loud whistle blows and a chugging noise begins.
The train starts slowly and then it gathers speed.
The journey is long and exciting.
It went through a dark, dark tunnel.
Soon we were there.
Everyone gets out of the train and goes home.

Matthew Labdon (8)
Monteclefe CE VA Junior School

AEROPLANE

There is a crackling noise on the aeroplane,
It starts flying from an airport.
It's very comfortable inside.
The aeroplane is exciting,
It goes up into the sky.
You start the engine.
It takes a long time to get to places.
The colours are silver, blue and red.
The aeroplane looks like a silver bird.
When you start to fly it is a bit bumpy.
It is slow and then it gets faster
It makes a loud noise.

Jessica Cox (7)
Monteclefe CE VA Junior School

THE RALLY CAR

The rally car is like a glaring, shot of thunder.
Its fierce wheels twist and turn.
Slushing dirt on its lovely shiny coat.
It's smooth and vibrating.
Crashing and bashing into white painted walls.
The windscreen wipers going back and forth
Working to clean the screen.
It speeds and gambles round tackling the cars
As it turns the corner.
Slower and slower and slower.
It runs over the finish line.
Its red and blue coat shines in the sunshine.
Hearing the crowd clapping before him.
He's the star of the whole race.

Anna Treece (8)
Monteclefe CE VA Junior School

WAYS TO TRAVEL

You can travel through the air,
You can travel underground.
If you have an accident,
You go spinning round and round.
Go zooming down the motorway,
On country roads a horse goes neigh.
Plane lights flash like the moonlight
And the fast flying jets get up to a terrible height.
Most important are our precious own feet
And children race to get the first seat.
You could always scoot to school,
Then go diving in the pool.

Catherine Honor (8)
Monteclefe CE VA Junior School

THE JET SKI

The engine roars while it glistens in the scorching hot sun.
It's my red dazzling jet ski.
I'm off.
Through the turquoise - blue clear water.
The speed gradually builds up.
A 1000 miles per hour red jet ski.
Skimming its way across the water.
Like a red dart.
Spraying froth everywhere.
Night falls.
I turn back.
At last I'm home.
I say goodnight.
In I go.

Archie Oram (7)
Monteclefe CE VA Junior School

SUBMARINE

My golden painted submarine
Is going through the sea,
Passing sharks and lobsters, fish and crabs,
And seeing things to see.

The ships above have no idea
What's sailing underneath.
But beneath the waves it sails
Once more,
Exploring and searching
The ocean floor.

Daniel Gardner (9)
Monteclefe CE VA Junior School

JOURNEYS

You can travel in car, you can travel by train,
You can travel in peace or travel in pain,
You can travel on animal or on feet,
Boats travel alone or in a fleet,
You can travel in helicopter or in plane,
You can travel in sunlight or in the rain,
You can travel in space with a spacecraft,
You can travel through water on a raft,
You can travel up high in a hot air balloon,
You can travel in a rocket up to the moon,
You travel when you walk or when you run,
Travelling can be really fun!

Isaac Skirton (9)
Monteclefe CE VA Junior School

RACING CAR

My racing car is fast.
It zooms like the wind.
It makes my hair zoom back.
I am second in the race.
There is a crash.
Oh no! Somebody else is winning,
I got ahead of him.
There is the finish line,
I have *won.*
Hooray!
I go to get the cup.

Felix Ho (7)
Monteclefe CE VA Junior School

MY HORSE, SAPPHIRE, SHE HAS SAPPHIRE EYES

We start from the stable, going into the countryside.
I tack up Sapphire, we walk . . . we start to trot . . . we go into
Canter then we gallop.
I hold the reins I hear her biting her bit.
I feel the soft, cool breeze running through my flying hair.
Sapphire's mane is waving, her tail is flying too.
I always say she's as fit as a racehorse.
Her fringe is blowing back.
She's pure black, she's shining in the sunlight.
Her hooves are black too.
'She's a big horse,' people say as we gallop past them.
We slow down to a canter and go into a trot.
I grip the leather saddle as we go through a river.
She's a fun horse - she's a super horse too.
Gently Sapphire plods on still in a canter,
We get to a field, we gallop across it.
We get to a little stream, we jump it then we find ourselves
Creeping into a forest.
We quickly gallop through.
I slow down and trot back to the stable.

Jessica Taylor (8)
Monteclefe CE VA Junior School

THE RABBIT

My rabbit is black and white,
With a brown smudge on her nose.
She is very, very cute
And has tiny little toes.
Her name is Spot,
And I love her a lot.

She hops about the garden
Leaving tiny little footprints
When the ground is wet.
She eats carrots and cabbage
And she nibbles all day.

Alice Cove (9)
Monteclefe CE VA Junior School

RIDING AN ELEPHANT DOWN THE STREET

My elephant is very dusty,
My elephant is light brown,
My elephant's got white tusks,
My elephant is like a brown stone.

I'm on my elephant now,
I'm bumping all around.
I'm all wibbly, wobbly,
I'm feeling very high.

I can see some tangly leaves,
I can see a dandelion,
I can see a tangerine,
I can see a sweet, sweety shop.

I'm travelling to the shop now
I'm feeling very hot.
I'm going in a puddle now,
I'm wet, spish spash, the elephant's wet.

I'm going home now,
I've got two miles to go.
I've got one mile to go
But now I'm safe and cosy in my house.

Jade Farmer (9)
Monteclefe CE VA Junior School

THE CAMEL

The camel's humpy
The camel's bumpy
Taking his journey
Through the dusty desert,
Trying to find some cool water.

The camel's hot
Like a boiling pot,
With eyes like black cauldrons,
His coat like the golden sun.

The camel's feet like
Crusty meat,
Walking through the bitty sand,
On the lumpy land.

The camel spits
A little bit.
His hooves like shiny silver ten pences.
I would like to know!
If he likes snow?
For he lives in the dusty desert.

Sophie-Mae Burgess (9)
Monteclefe CE VA Junior School

CAR

Twinkling windows.
Speeding fast.
Shining red paint.
Dark black tyres.
Shining headlights.

Zach Ball (8)
Monteclefe CE VA Junior School

THE PLANE

The plane starts up.
Starting to move forward.
It picks up speed.
It takes off into the sky.
Higher and higher.
Up and up into the sky.
Doing the loop the loop.
It tilts itself.
It is fast, noisy and exciting.
The white flight building is wobbling in the wind.
The windows are nice and clear.
A puff of smoke comes out of the back.
Out flies a sackful of soot.
The motor is burning and breaking.
The plane is diving and twisting.
Down and down and down.
Into the sea.
People and plane disappear under the waves.

Stephen Attwood (7)
Monteclefe CE VA Junior School

CAR

Shooting round the corner,
A fast red fireball.
Circling around the roundabout.
Speeding like a shooting star.
5000mph on the M5.
Takes over every motor car.
The furious sports car.
Going faster and faster.
As dirty as a hippo.

Bradley Baxter (7)
Monteclefe CE VA Junior School

The Wandering Hag

Old and crinkly is the horrible hag,
Who wanders to and fro,
And if ever you meet the wandering hag,
Your tales will be of woe!

Travelling on mouldy feet,
She travels to hag land,
And if she meets a wolf so fierce,
It will be lying in the sand!

As she travels in all weathers,
Hoping she'll be there,
Sore on her wart covered feet,
She has a poisonous glare.

Finally she's there at last,
Eviler with her spells,
But beware when she comes back here,
There'll be some piercing yells.

Frances Foyne (9)
Monteclefe CE VA Junior School

The Pony Ride

I am a pony in a field
My fur is toffee-brown.
Patiently I wait
For my rider to ride me.
I run round the field,
With my glimmering, shiny eyes.

My trainer rides me every day,
To see how I do.
I want to join my friends
In the obstacle race.

At the end of the day
When I've had a good play
I join the rest in the stable,
Hoping I am with them next time.

Jordan Chambers (9)
Monteclefe CE VA Junior School

THE SPORTS CAR

Its flames burn fiercely behind it.
Ready for it.
Ready for the race.
A beeping . . .
The green lights are beeping . . .
Off it goes!
Faster and faster,
Speeding round all the corners
Eighty miles an hour
Its shiny red metal glittering in the sunlight.
There it is . . .
The finish line.
Only two feet away.
One foot away.
He's done it
He's won.
The crowd is cheering like mad.
Clapping and clapping.
It's as loud as a building falling over.
The driver says
'Thank you everybody, thank you.'

Alex Tallon (8)
Monteclefe CE VA Junior School

THE CAR

The engine starts fast and off it goes.
In the distance gets faster and faster.
Off it goes through the trees,
Faster and faster.
Through the field it goes, faster and faster.
Through the forest it goes, faster and faster.
It gets near to the finish line,
1000 miles an hour, he is in first place.
He wins. He says yes! yes! I won the race.
Everyone cheers and he is happy, really happy.
Really happy because he won the race.
First place.

Carl Cawley (7)
Monteclefe CE VA Junior School

TORTOISE

A browny green tortoise,
Struggling trying to reach his target.
The other end of the garden.
Tugging and pulling his liney oval shell.
His diamond eyes sparkling in the gleaming sunshine.
Try to graduate his speed.
Plodding along going as fast as he can.
The big wet chipped wall,
Drying slowly in the hot reddy orangey sun.
Just then the owner comes
And picks up the heavy tortoise.

Rebecca Elliott (7)
Monteclefe CE VA Junior School

THE AEROPLANE

The engine runs,
The wheels start going round . . .
It bumps up and down.
The floor feels bumpy.
It flies in the clouds.
It looks like a silver bird with silver wings.
People travel in the plane to fly.
It takes off and blasts off,
Over the fluffy clouds.
The sun shines on the plane.
Its as shiny as disco top.
It starts to land.

Chloe Burton (7)
Monteclefe CE VA Junior School

BOAT

I cast my beautiful net in the heart of the sea.
I'm very proud of my blue and red boat.
My blue and red rectangular boat.
I'm very, very proud.
My blue and red boat is small but fast.
We're going round a corner very, very slow.
This boat has a built in radio.
Its top speed is 48 miles an hour.
The sun is setting, time for me to go.
I'm casting off towards the beautiful shore.
The fish I've caught are blue and gold.

Sam Almond (7)
Monteclefe CE VA Junior School

TRAIN

The shiny red and blue carriage
Chugging along the track.
Quickly trotting to the station.
People are waiting quietly for the red and blue shining train.
You hear the noisy engine
Chugging from a mile away.
There it is glistening in the sunshine.
All the people up on the platform
Amazed as it comes into the station.
All the passengers get onto the glistening carriages.
On every green velvet seat are beautiful gold numbers.
It starts to trot out of the station.
It chugs slowly
Then a bit faster
Faster still.
Going into the countryside.
Chugging on and on and on
Bobbing along the track
Hooting through all the tunnels
Station to station.
Passing lots of sights
Gardens,
Washing lines,
Deer.
Everyone is watching
Staring at us all.

Carla Tate (8)
Monteclefe CE VA Junior School

THE PLANE

The engine starts.
The aeroplane rises from the airport.
You wave goodbye to your dad.
The plane takes speed.
Faster and faster.
The aeroplane is silver, red and blue.
You can hear the crackling of the radio.
The aeroplane starts to bump.
Up and down bumpity bump the aeroplane goes.
The aeroplane arrives at the airport.

Kieren Moncur (8)
Monteclefe CE VA Junior School

BOAT

When the boat goes out in the water
The fish go away.
They are scared.
They are sad.
They see the boat coming.
They know they will get caught.
The boat is red and shiny.
The net is brown and grey.
Quickly the fish swim away.

Thomas May (7)
Monteclefe CE VA Junior School

A FISH

A lovely fish,
Look it is gold and orange.
It is going down a wonderful waterfall.
Let's follow it.
Come on, let's go.
It is going faster.
It is getting slower.
Come on.

Cassie Brown (8)
Monteclefe CE VA Junior School

FERRARI

The jet black Ferrari standing on the drive.
Happily it starts to go
100 miles per hour.
It zooms down the road.
Out into the countryside.
The sun starts to set.
It shines on the paint.

James Plowman (8)
Monteclefe CE VA Junior School

CHEETAH

Quick, fast, lazy cheetah
Hiding in the grass
Sneaking up on its prey
Zebras fleeing in terror.

Smart, swift and sleek
Difficult to see
Crouching in the bush
Very quietly.

Rapid, briskly, speedy
Hidden by the grasses
Hard to see
Good camouflage.

Chloe Parchment (9)
North Newton CP School

WHITE WITCHES, MIDNIGHT HOUR

White witches gliding silently,
Half an hour 'til midnight.
Their cats wailing noisily,
Half an hour 'til midnight.
The witches chatter quietly,
Half an hour 'til midnight.
Black shadows on the ground,
Half an hour 'til midnight.
One witch leads the way,
Quarter of an hour 'til midnight.
The patter of feet on moonlight hill,
Ten minutes 'til midnight.
The witches are waiting silently,
Five minutes 'til midnight.
Some cats are purring loudly,
Three minutes 'til midnight.
Two minutes 'til midnight.
One minute 'til midnight.
Hooray, hooray, it's midnight at last
Let the celebrations begin.

Gemma Hogg (11)
North Newton CP School

people say don't so much?
'Don't bite your nails.'
'Don't tease the dog with food when it's in a bad mood.'
'Don't pour beer in your brother's ear.'
'Don't pour more in Mum's bedroom door.'
'Don't put your foot in the soot.'
'Don't kick Rich in the lip.'
'Don't keep saying won't.'
'Don't sit on your sister's swimming kit.'
'Don't swim in the moat.'
'Don't take the rake and throw it in the lake.'
'Don't make Grandpa wake.'
So why do people say don't so much?

Arran Watkins (10)
North Newton CP School

THE GREEDY DOG

I once saw a greedy dog
Walking in a misty fog
He was looking for some food
But he could not find any and got in a bad mood
He was walking for hours
But all he could find was flowers
Then he saw some soup
That turned out to be an old tin
When he saw some corn
It turned out to be dawn
He went to the river and saw some fish
He wanted some food that was his wish.

Thomas Cottey (10)
North Newton CP School

MIDNIGHT BLACK MAGIC

At midnight one night,
With no one in sight
A witch cast a spell.

> She had a black cat
> That sat on her hat,
> With a long, black, shiny tail.

The witch made a potion
And had no notion
That she would now rule the world.

> She added a few bats' legs
> And a couple of snakes' eggs,
> And the cauldron was bubbling over.

A mist covered the surface
Of the sparkling water
While everything crackled.

> A broomstick stood in the corner
> And it was outlined with cobwebs for a border
> Black hairy spiders creeping around.

It was full moon
And as light shined in,
Boom! The witch was sucked into her potion.

> Never to be seen again.

Sophie Carney (11)
North Newton CP School

WINTER

It is winter
It is cold up on the hill,
Snow falls there still.
There is no movement except for the beautiful herd of wild ponies
They have silky, smooth coats keeping the nasty chill out
They love to prance about.

It is winter
A fox creeps silently through the trees
Ready to seize its prey
A robin sits in a tree of snow and watches the world go by.

It is winter
Some deer are at the river, splashing
Rabbits are in their burrows too
It is night time and the world is in darkness until another day.

Charlotte Foster (9)
North Newton CP School

THE DRAGON

The dragon flying high, soaring above the treetops
Breathing fire from its flaming mouth
Slicing through his prey with his razor-sharp claws
His hard, horny hide is more than a match for bullets, swords and spears
His large splayed feet crush anything in his path.

His flaming eyes bring fear to even the bravest knight or warrior.
I wouldn't like to meet him
Myth or legend.

Shaun Cook (9)
North Newton CP School

MY PUPPY

My puppy is cuddly
He can run very fast
But if he runs with me he is always last.

My puppy is smooth
He is always wet
He is a great comfort
My puppy is the best pet.

My puppy plays a lot
He eats more than he plays
He plays with his ball
Turns night into days.

My puppy is so muddy
He chases the rabbits that get in his way
If you let him go with you he'll always whine but stay.

Maria Perry (8)
North Newton CP School

FIREWORKS

F   izzling fireworks
I   like to see
R   ed fireworks
E   verywhere
W   hirling, banging, crashing
O   range
R   ed
K   eeping me fascinated
S   izzling fireworks spread across the sky!

Rosie Anholt (9)
North Newton CP School

AMBUSH

The dinosaur was hiding in the bushes
The moonlight shone on his eyes
Food was fifty metres in front of him
The hunger had got to him
As he is looking
Snap!
The little dinosaurs ran as fast as they can
The bigger dinosaur goes after them
But . . .
They are too fast.

Jake Burroughs (11)
North Newton CP School

FIREWORKS

F   ountains sizzling
I   wait with great excitement
R   ed and blue and green
E   verything is quiet
W   riggling, popping fireworks
O   range and yellow, purple and pink
R   ockets and Roman candles
K   eeping me wide-eyed
S   creeching and crackling.

Rebecca Coram (10)
North Newton CP School

THE OCEAN

The ocean is beautiful with lots of flowers on the seabed
                         and lots of dolphins and fish and a boat.
The ocean is like you're standing on the sky but without any clouds.
The ocean can roar like a tiger hunting for its prey.
The ocean is like you're on a different planet.
The ocean smells like a cake mix in the kitchen that has just been made.
The ocean tastes like orange juice poured into apple juice.
It looks like lots of people wearing blue swimming costumes.

Bethany Cude (7)
North Petherton Junior School

THE VOLCANO

A volcano is like a burning cheetah running down a mountain.
A volcano lava is like a red-hot gunge smashing the tree.
A volcano is like a dusty shelf which is never cleaned.
A volcano is like a bear roaring in the wind.
A volcano sounds like huge waves crashing against
                                    the cliffs on the shore.
A volcano looks like a burning forest fire in the sky.

Joseph Ellis (8)
North Petherton Junior School

THE FIRE

Fire is like you are burning in a grave and like you are fainting in terror.
Fire sounds like an eagle attacking a cliff and a dragon
                                    breathing fire fiercely.
Fire looks like blood dripping down mountains and cockroaches
                                    appearing from mid-air.

Bethan Langridge (8)
North Petherton Junior School

OCEAN

The ocean's waves crash on islands like a stampede of elephants falling
                                                          from the sky.
The ocean is as blue as the sky.
The oceans drown islands like a plant falling in a black hole.
The ocean burns fire like the sun burning Pluto.
The ocean destroys electric like gas tanks exploding.
The ocean's icebergs destroy boats like us stepping on an ant.

Beau Ingram (7)
North Petherton Junior School

THE EARTHQUAKE

Earthquake is like a dish when I drop it to the ground
                                          tearing the flats apart.
The earthquake looks like pointed sticks and tears like a bear.
The earthquake shakes the world all around.
Earthquake sounds like a dragon roaring.
An earthquake shakes like a lion with its prey.
An earthquake laughs like a giant monster.

Jack Curtis (8)
North Petherton Junior School

THE EARTHQUAKE

The earthquake is like someone tearing a piece of paper apart.
An earthquake is like someone shaking the Earth.
An earthquake makes the Earth wail and cry like a baby crying.
An earthquake tears the houses down.
When the earthquake knocks down trees it is like someone pulling
                              vegetables from a soft warm soil bed.

Alice Michieli (8)
North Petherton Junior School

THE FOREST

The dark, gloomy forest has sounds of terror screeching all around you
with bats flying everywhere.
It smells like socks that have not been washed and rotten eggs
And wolves howls and the wind rushing through the trees rustling
the trees' leaves.
It rushes through the lovely, lush green grass.
There is dark all around you
You are like a star floating in the sky.

James Fox (8)
North Petherton Junior School

THE FIRE

The fire is like a dragon's hot rage
It uses its hot flames to tear forest like a chainsaw cutting down trees.
Burning, it blazes like a dragon's flame-thrower.

The fire is a dragon's rapid flame with a big swipe to terrorise forest.
The fire is a volcano moving and laying eggs and crashing
with nothing inside.
The fire is an earthquake of blazing boulders.

Matthew Warne (7)
North Petherton Junior School

THE FIRE

The fire is like blood and lava erupting from a volcano.
The fire is like hot chilli bubbling in your mouth.
The fire is like red gas and boiling hot water in a kettle.
Fire is roaring as fierce as a lion.

Kelly Parker (8)
North Petherton Junior School

HAPPY

Happy is yellow.
It tastes like meat
And smells like flowers.
It looks like beautiful grass
And sounds like Jessica calling for me.
It makes me feel like I want to play.

Amy Duddridge (7)
North Petherton Junior School

HAPPINESS

It tastes like chocolate
And smells like roast chicken.
It looks like people playing
And sounds like people playing in the park.
It makes me feel nice.

Andrew Clark (8)
North Petherton Junior School

HAPPY

Yellow is happy.
It tastes like a Fruit Pastel
And smells like puppies
And sounds like Amy.
It makes me feel great.

Jessica Webber (7)
North Petherton Junior School

FIRE

The fire is like hot chillies bubbling in your mouth.
The red-hot fire tears down all the greenness and logs in the forest.
The young, boiling, hot fire turns to grey and white ash with old age.
The blazing fire chews through the forest.
The spiky, red-hot fire is like dripping red blood.
The red glowing fire spits through things.
Fire roars with the fierceness of a lion.

Laura Baker (8)
North Petherton Junior School

THE FLY

I wonder where the flies go
I often stop to think
Do they fly away and die
Or stop in some small chink.

They are big and black and hairy
And buzz around the room
Up and down the walls
Quickly duck here's one coming . . . zoom.

They are quick and clever
And difficult to catch
But when they are near me
They have met their match.

If I had all day
I would squat them flat.
If they are back again
I would definitely wear a hat.

Bethany Manders (9)
St Aldhelm's CE Primary School, Shepton Mallet

THE BIG OLD HOUSE

Old house, dusty house,
Old house, big house,
Have you got lots of room?

Old house, spooky house,
Old house, cobwebby house,
Yes I have lots of room!

Old house, dirty house,
Old house, dark house,
Can I move in?

Old house, broken floorboard house,
Old house, broken glass house,
Of course you can!

Old house, warm house,
Old house, cosy house,
I'm moving in!

Louisa Garbett (8)
St Aldhelm's CE Primary School, Shepton Mallet

MY OLD BIKE

Old bike, old bike,
Rusty and dirty.
Old bike, old bike,
Funny and dirty.
Old bike, old bike,
Squeaky and broke.
Old bike, old bike,
My old bike.

Gemma Carver (9)
St Aldhelm's CE Primary School, Shepton Mallet

TEACHERS

Teachers are great
With lots on their plate.
One gives me books
He has charming looks
He goes quite bold
'Do as you're told!'
One is short
Who will be brought to Nottingham
With her special man
She might put gel pens to a ban.
Mr Knowles is an expert at DT
So let's finish the day
With biscuits and tea.

Zoë Barnes (10)
St Aldhelm's CE Primary School, Shepton Mallet

MY COSY BED

My bed,
My bed,
I love my bed,
Warm and cosy
Comfy head.
Teddies sitting at the end,
Always want to be my friend.
Pillows plump,
Blankets warm,
I'm happy there
From dusk 'til dawn.

Esme Stevens (9)
St Aldhelm's CE Primary School, Shepton Mallet

BOOKS

You find books everywhere
I come across them everyday
Every time I look around I find them,
Under the stairs for boots to trample.
On my bed for sweet dreams,
In the attic for ghosts to read, and
Up the stairs because the stairs get bored.
Books, books, books,
I find them everyday
Because what I have been trying to tell you
All the time you see
Is that you really do find books absolutely
Everywhere!

Nicola Pillinger (9)
St Aldhelm's CE Primary School, Shepton Mallet

OUT IN SPACE

As you're flying through the sky
Lots of shooting stars go by
When comets speed past your ship
Your spacecraft has to dip and dive to get out of the way
Metallic satellites shine in the ray of the sun
There is the moon cold as ice
Someone's on it
You can see
It's an astronaut
Waving at me.

Ben Neale (10)
St Aldhelm's CE Primary School, Shepton Mallet

MONSTER IN THE CLOSET

Monster in the closet
What a dreadful sight
Left a big deposit
In the middle of the night.

Monster in the closet
Heard but never seen
Don't know where he went to
Only I know where he's been.

Monster in the closet
Almost made me cry
Made the time to say hello
But never said goodbye.

Charlotte Mair (8)
St Aldhelm's CE Primary School, Shepton Mallet

MY DOG

She's crazy with her toys
Just like boys.

Growling at her toys thinking they're alive
Sounds like a bee hive.

We go heave
When she pulls on the lead.

She loves running
And her tail does the drumming.

My dog is crazy
And she is lazy.

Samantha Fry (8)
St Aldhelm's CE Primary School, Shepton Mallet

THE NINE PLANETS

There are nine planets
Orbiting the sun,
But the sun is quite still
Burning with gases.

The sun is out there
Burning and boiling with gases.

The biggest of all the planets is Jupiter
Next to Saturn
Next is strange Uranus,
Then all the rest.

Tiny Pluto is furthest of all
Baking Venus is the hottest.

The nine strange planets orbit the sun.

Vincent Wood Johnson (7)
St Aldhelm's CE Primary School, Shepton Mallet

DRAGONS

The dragon is the strongest link in The Weakest Link show
With his scales dropping slowly to the floor.
He is a mysterious moonless cave
He is the sweat of a girl's nightmare
Earthquakes come as he stomps
His teeth are as sharp as razor blades
He sorts out his problem on the Ricki Lake Show.
His eyes are a blazing, blinding yellow
With pupils as red as bubbling lava.
His snore is the thunder as he sleeps.

Alex Duchezeau (11)
St Aldhelm's CE Primary School, Shepton Mallet

IF I HAD WINGS . . .

If I had wings . . .
I would swoop and glide over the green, green fields.

I would fly among fairies visiting the flowers.

I would skim the sky.

I would touch the tips of the night sky's diamonds.

I would dash round Jupiter's ring one thousand times each day.

I would rest within the crescent and eat the moonlight and kiss
the edge of day.

Lily Haggart (9)
St Aldhelm's CE Primary School, Shepton Mallet

MY WEIRD DOG

When Shandy licks, her tongue is filled with slime,
And Shandy licks all the time.

When Shandy plays she likes to bark at you
And I like to bark back too.

When Shandy's sick she licks it up after,
And I just have to cry with laughter.

She jumps on the coffee table and takes our food
But only when she gets in a mood.

Suzy Corner (8)
St Aldhelm's CE Primary School, Shepton Mallet

THE RABBIT

There was once a rabbit looking at me
I stared at him and I could see
He was humming and humming all day long
He just sat there and sang a song
Today is my birthday and I could see
That same rabbit staring at me.

Fiona Stevens (7)
St Aldhelm's CE Primary School, Shepton Mallet

POOR MOG

There was a young cat called Mog
Who always set off for a jog
It caused lots of fights
And sometimes a fright
Because of the next door's dog.

Thomas Patterson (10)
St Aldhelm's CE Primary School, Shepton Mallet

LOVE

Love is the colour of a red rose
A rich and sweet smell of flowers
It feels of soft velvet,
But unlike the rose, love lasts forever.

Jessica Wilkins (10)
St Aldhelm's CE Primary School, Shepton Mallet

THE PIRATE ADVENTURE

In a land far away, sailed a ship called Mary Jay
It sailed the open seas, to look for enemies.

The leader was One-Eyed Jack
With a parrot on his back.

One stormy night
He gave himself a fright.
The boat hit a giant wave,
That sent it into a secret cave.

Captain Jack and his crew,
Didn't know what to do.

They got out the rum
And waited for the sun to rise
To light up the cave
What a surprise!

There was gold, silver and coins shimmering in the light.

The pirates loaded the boat with treasure
Their faces gleamed with pleasure.

All loaded up and ready to go,
They left the cave on the crest of a wave,
Homeward bound, safe and sound.

Robert Trick (10)
St Aldhelm's CE Primary School, Shepton Mallet

IN THE JUNGLE WHAT DO I SEE?

Its skin is orange and black
It eats deer and it's ready to attack
It is gliding through the jungle
It is climbing up a tree
First I look and then I see
It is coming after me!

Stephanie Walters (7)
St Aldhelm's CE Primary School, Shepton Mallet

A JOURNEY TO SPACE

A journey to space is a very weird place
So you have to be very careful.
But what is that I see flying in the air?
It looks like a big brown bear,
A journey to space is very weird,
And now I think I am growing a beard!
I start to moan and groan,
Now I think it is definitely time to go home.

Joel Pope (8)
St John's RC School, Bath

A CAR JOURNEY

In the car on the way to school
I stop and stare at the houses
Sometimes they're big, sometimes they're small
But really they are all the same.

Theo Brand (8)
St John's RC School, Bath

MY DINOSAUR FRIEND

I live in a tree so no one can make fun of me
I ride on a blood eating monster
He is my friend
T-Rex is a carnivore
He's quite nice
What does he eat?
I know meat and big feet of course and there's a lot of heat
Look there's a swamp
Quickly dive there's a bee hive
Quickly run home
Phew!

Eilis Barrett (7)
St John's RC School, Bath

TIME TRAVEL

I'm bored,
I'll go to the shops,
I'll buy the time machine I saw yesterday
This is exciting.
I'm confused, how do you use it?
I'll read the instruction manual
I told my friends I've got a time machine
When I tried it out it was sure cool.
I was a bit worried before I tried it
Once I got lost in time but I got back home.
My mum and dad want me to sell it
I was sad
My friend's got one now
I felt mad.

Rowland Goodbody (8)
St John's RC School, Bath

HOLIDAY POEM

I want to go away
On a charming holiday.
I will never be a boaster
If I go on that rollercoaster
And if we go to Spain
It will never rain.
I will go again
And I'll never complain,
To go to Spain.

Bella Emery (8)
St John's RC School, Bath

THE GOLDEN SEA

I can see the golden sea,
It's pretty and shiny.
I can see the golden sea,
It's shining at me.
I can see the golden sea,
It shines very brightly.
I love the golden sea.

Bethan Gray (8)
St John's RC School, Bath

FLYING HIGH

Flying high in the sky
Being sick on my dish
Feeling ill, take a pill
Yippee . . . tee hee
Flying high in the sky.

James Indoe (8)
St John's RC School, Bath

BACK IN TIME

I am ill, I need to take a pill
We have a rocket, it has a pocket
How do we get in the rocket?
Of course we jump in the pocket
How do we control these things, there are lots of controls?
Which one?

Demelza Watkins
St John's RC School, Bath

SPACE

5, 4, 3, 2, 1, blast-off
Oh it's very noisy
Oh Mars, Pluto and the Milky Way
Is it me or am I seeing Twix and KitKat?
Nah that isn't a space thing
I'm boiling aaarrrhhh - the sun
Better put on the brakes
Snap!

Thomas Southcott (8)
St John's RC School, Bath

IN THE SEA

In the sea you see the fish and wish that you were deeper
When you go deeper you see the shark. Oh no!
Hide behind the bark.
Swim deeper, see the whale. Oh no! I've gone pale
Swim up to the surface, I'm cold, let's go home.

Thomas Prangley (8)
St John's RC School, Bath

THE WORLD GONE WRONG

War is over here,
War is over there,
Oh when does it stop?
Because my feelings are in a fright
As my friends and family fight
While I sit by the window and pray.

I watch the world go wrong
While love ones fight for so long
Guns are shot, bombs are thrown
Bullets hit people, bombs kill
While the enemies are in thrill.

Rejoice, the war is over
But pain as I found cat who's dead
My father's dead but they gave me his lead
So I can remember him as if he is alive.

I buy a poppy to respect who died
And who are still alive.
This is the world gone wrong.

Hazel Walker (10)
St John's RC School, Bath

SPEED BOAT

It is cool.
It goes zooming past me.
It is black and red and it is waterproof.
It is fast.
It is faster than a car.
It makes a noise.
It has got a black tyre.

Brenden King (8)
St John's RC School, Bath

SPACE ROCKETS

The space is like a hole
It is white up to the North Pole.

S   pace is so calm
P   eople jumping arm in arm
A   nd men going up in rockets
C   an you see hands in pockets?
E   veryone loves space.

The space is like a black hole
It is white up to the North Pole.

R   ockets shooting up in space
O   ur people say they can see a face
C   ountdown starts before they're off
K   ilometres thousands away we go before the cough
E   veyrone cheers
T   he family has tears
S   o off we go.

The space is like a black hole
It is white up to the North Pole.

Lucy Baker (11)
St John's RC School, Bath

THE SWORD AND SHIELD

In the old medieval times there was evil and loads of crimes
The very best killer was the blade
He's quite thin and not insane.

His sister the shield is just as annoying
It simply stops blows and ceases destroying.

Jim Chalmers (10)
St John's RC School, Bath

KEEPER OF THE SUN AND MOON

A creature prowls the midnight sky
Silhouetted against the moon
Born of fire, it came from the Earth
The dragon spirit of the night.

Its breath brings shadows
And calls out the moon
It soars to the heavens
And daylight is gone.

But night cannot last
And with one final burst
This dragon breathes fire
And swallows the moon.

The fire takes shape
To a bright burning orb
For though we feel no time has passed
The dragon has felt it all.

Joseph O'Hara (10)
St John's RC School, Bath

POETIC VOYAGE

I step up to the ship
The port is as blank as my mind,
I pull up the sail
Ready to set off.
The wheel is rusty as I turn it,
It creeks, a rusty noise
I am on a voyage of no return
Where will I go?
Says a whisper in the wind.

Lauren Jones (10)
St John's RC School, Bath

PIRATES

My brother and I play pirates
We play it every day
We always use our beds as ships
'Ahoy me mate' we say.

We set sail towards the ocean
As captain smuggler I say
'We've got ourselves some stowaways
Who won't live another day!'

I climbed up to the crow's nest
'Land ahoy!' I say
'Ahoy me fellow scallywags.
We'll fight another day!'

Michael Corkhill (11)
St John's RC School, Bath

DRAGON TEARS

A forest.
Inside the forest is . . .
Grass.
Under the grass is . . .
A cave.
Inside the cave are . . .
Jewels.
Under the jewels is . . .
A dragon.
Inside the dragon are . . .
Feelings.
Inside the feelings are . . .
Dragon tears.

Rosie Dunn (9)
St John's RC School, Bath

TEENAGERS

'Mum can I have a phone?'
'Shut up and go home.'
'But that isn't fair.'
'Shut up I don't care.'

'But all my friends are coming here.'
'I know but you won't be here.'
'Oh yes I will.' 'Oh no you won't.
You're going home, grab your coat.'

'All I want is a friend and a phone.'
'It gives you brain damage and makes you moan.'
'But what about my friends?'
'It's a school night that has to end.'

'Hey mates.'
'Hey Kate.'
'Let's go somewhere else.'
'Good idea, Shelse.'

Laura Goodbody (10)
St John's RC School, Bath

GUESS WHO?

Play producer,
Theatre user,
Song maker,
Heart breaker,
Poetry inventor,
Romeo and Juliet creator.

It's Shakespeare.

Sofia Pavan (10)
St John's RC School, Bath

A DRAGON

A breeze came through my window
I went to shut my window
And at the same time a dragon came to mind
And a roar was heard.

I slipped my dressing gown on
And grabbed a torch
I crept down the stairs and out the door
Turned the light on.

Looked round the corner
I looked about the tree
And another roar was heard
I heard it coming from the oak tree.

And there I found
A dragon's head coming out of the hole
Me and him crept into the house and up the stairs
I kept him as a pet
He lived under my bed.

Katie Benjamin (10)
St John's RC School, Bath

HIGH FLIGHT

The golden-tipped wings of a Spitfire
The shiny sun making shadows on the clouds.
Flying like a hawk
Looking for prey
I dive, I swoop, I drop
I feel I've touched God.

James Creese (9)
St John's RC School, Bath

STORM CLOUDS GATHER

Storm clouds slash, storm clouds boom, storm clouds gather.

Whistling, wheezing, whining, whoosh,
Screeching round the corner.
Creaking, striking the battered door,
The rusty hinges cry for mercy from the wretched wind!

Storm clouds slash, storm clouds boom, storm clouds gather.

Pitter, patter . . . streak, clitter, clatter,
Lightening jagged against a rough silky bark tree.
Boom the thunder takes over.
A constant argument!

Storm clouds slash, storm clouds boom, storm clouds gather.

Thomas Rowland (9)
St John's RC School, Bath

DRAGONS EAT TOO MUCH

In the far corner of the Earth there was a dragon who ate too much
And here is what he ate
Flies wings with nibbled earwigs
And for tea he had mushed caterpillars.

When it was September the 5th
All the dragons from the corners of the world would meet
And they had a feast
It was a big feast of beetle's legs and human's bones to chew on.
That was the start and the sight that I shuddered with spite
                                          on a horrible night.

Nicholas Kapetanakis (9)
St John's RC School, Bath

FEAR IS . . .

Fear tastes like fire burning in your mouth
Or fear feels like hot beans jumping in your hand.

Fear smells like smelly socks pinned to your nose
Or fire burning in a big forest.

Fear feels scary like a dark room where you don't know

                              what will happen

Or a slimy snail on your hand.

Fear sounds like an owl hooting in the night
Or a person shouting very loudly.

Fear looks like a black spider,
A spiky, black spider crawling up your long legs.

Rebecca Proctor (10)
St John's RC School, Bath

HIGH FLIGHT

The sun beating down on your cockpit
The clouds as white as cotton wool or screwed up pieces of paper.

The giant towns from down low look so tiny from up here.

You think you've left your stomach in your house.

Gliding through the sky you think you're sitting on a bird.

You think the enemy is breathing down your neck.

Then it's all black, down and down into bottomless pit for ever, ever.

Anthony McLaughlin (10)
St John's RC School, Bath

THE MOVEMENT ON THE SHIP

The sea moves up and down
And comes aboard the ship.

The wind blows in my face
And my hair blows in my eyes.

The ship would rock on the waves
It would throw you side to side.

The rain feels very heavy
It would splash in my face.

Then out the sun would come
And the waves would disappear.

And then we would set sail again
And all of us would start to cheer.

Laura Stevenson (10)
St John's RC School, Bath

IN SPACE

Space is a big place
And dark and gloomy
And it has got a lot of space.

Planets and comets race
Each other until they win
In space.

And the stars shine bright
At each other
In the dark night.

Aidan Kalsi (8)
St John's RC School, Bath

DRAGON NIGHT

D ragons fly high in the sky
R ed fire is what they breathe
A bove our heads they sweep
G oing up into the dark night sky
O ver towns and hills
N ight after night they fly high
S ilently he walks through the air.

D ragon flies high in the night
R aging and roaring flying by the starlight sky
A bove their tails sway side to side
G oing past the starlight sky, higher and higher
O ver the stars and the moon
N icely floating back home past the stars
S ilently he goes back to his hiding place.

Katie Thorpe (9)
St John's RC School, Bath

THE VIKING VOYAGE

I saw a Viking one day
I said 'Please go away'
'Where is your head?' I said
'Where is your bed?' he said.
'It's in my voyage boat, safe and sound
But I am shrinking into the ground.'
'Hey get out it's my ground.'
He smashed the ground
Sent me flying to homeward bound
To rest my head safe and sound.

Sidonie Travers (8)
St John's RC School, Bath

THE VIEW OF EARTH

In the bright light of the sun
In a small, fast aeroplane
I can see the ocean
Packed full with colourful fish
Sharks, whales and dolphins.

I can see mountains,
Snow mountains and grass mountains.
I can see the trees,
Big trees, leafy trees and small trees.
I can see buildings, schools
Shops, churches and markets.

I can see children
Lots of children, toddlers and babies.
I can see cars,
Lorries, buses and vans.
I can see birds, lots of birds,
Robins, blue tits and pigeons.

I can see animals
Foxes, tigers and lions.
I can see fields, fields with flowers,
Fields with food and fields with grass.
I can see everything up high
The view of Earth is fantastic.

Samuel Langley (10)
St John's RC School, Bath

DRAGON DREAM

As the moon became full
A shiver ran down my spine
I walked towards the old, mossy cave
Then I encountered it.
The crimson dragon.

Its flaky skin, shining in the moonlight
Then it saw me, I tried to hide
But still it could see me
Then it picked me up, I was in a panic.

But it did not hurt
It did not hurt
Like I thought it would
Not a scratch, not a bruise
Then he took me on a adventure
Through the windy trees
In and out of the moonlight.

I did not know why
Why he did not kill me
Why he did not devour me on the spot
Then he let out a fountain of flames
Red, orange and yellow
Then in a flurry of light
I was in my bed sleeping, slowly and silently.

William Fane-Gladwin (9)
St John's RC School, Bath

IN A PLANE

When I'm in an aeroplane
I can see lots of people playing on the beach
Some having a bathe and eating an ice cream.
I see people driving combine harvesters on a big farm.
I see goats and ducks being fed on a lovely sunny day at the zoo.
I see ambulances rescuing people because they're ill or have got hurt.
I see people playing in the park on the monkey bars and on the swings.
I see people making their garden better by putting flowers in it.
I see footballers playing a professional football match.
I see people having water fights on a hot sunny day
                                        in their back gardens.
I see buses, coaches, cars and other transport travelling to shops and
                                        other places.
I see children riding on their bikes.
I see builders building a house.

James Simmons (9)
St John's RC School, Bath

THE VOYAGE OF LIFE

Life is like a voyage across the sea
You're sailing smoothly and your life is going perfectly
Then a fierce storm approaches and something very bad happens
                                        in your life
Then you go smoothly again
Your journey is to dry land, a place of wonder
The journey will take many years
The years go by, the ship is damaged from the storms of your life
Then the ship finds dry land a place of wonder
It's over the voyage of life is over
You're in a better place.

Patrick Crook (10)
St John's RC School, Bath

DRAGON'S ROAR

Somewhere in my mind I see a dragon with green, ugly eyes
With red and orange fire.
I can feel it in my mind
My mind is spinning round and round
I feel it in my head
There's a baby dragon blowing bits of fire
Hitting each dragon roars as they fly around in the air
Catching each other with fireballs
Running on the floor, grabbing each other's tails.
Blowing fire and breaking stuff.
Dragon flying so high blowing fire in my mind
I can feel it blowing in my head
My mind hurt with lots of fire
My head is going to blow as I sleep in the dark caves.

Kimberley (10)
St John's RC School, Bath

THE VOYAGE ON THE SEA

Standing on the ship looking at the clear water
The waves gentle as we sail on them.
The wind blowing hard to push us
And the sea gently moving the boat from side to side.
The land is in sight, the wind blowing harder and making us faster.
The land two miles away.
A storm gathered, the rain smashing on the floor of the ship.
The rain stopping and the sun shining
We slowly pull to shore.
We get off quickly and what do you think we saw?

Nathan Hawkins (10)
St John's RC School, Bath

THE FLIGHT OF THE AEROPLANE

As I fly above the Earth
I start to see the bright, green turf
Then I see the deep, blue seas
The mountains, the buildings, the leafy trees,
Then I see the land, the grass
The city statue made of brass.
I also see the coloured cars
I look above and see the stars
I looked below, the aeroplane was really loud
And then I spotted a fluffy cloud.
Then I saw a church so big
You could clearly see it in a MiG.
I saw playing fields
A shop selling fishing reels
I see playgrounds
Lots of dirt in muddy mounds.
I see schools
With books about ghouls.
I sat there gazing
God's world is amazing.

Hugh Corkhill (9)
St John's RC School, Bath

HIGH FLIGHT

I am in an enormous plane
Now I can see some geese
And I think I can see the face of God
But is it true that the sun is the face of God?
But I am happy because I like going upside down
But goodbye for now.

Iona Lowery (9)
St John's RC School, Bath

MY VIEW OF EARTH

Up in the sunlit sky
Just hovering there
Looking down on Earth
I see the sea full of colourful fish
I see hundreds of towns
At least it seems.
The fields full of animals
And new born sheep.
The fields are full of crops,
How wonderful is this?
The hills connecting all the fields,
With flowers which make you happy.
I see mountains with people climbing them,
With chunks of snow on top.
I see the whole countryside
With cosy looking cottages.
The top of mountains
Peering through the mist.
I see orange deserts
Full of pyramids.

Ella Pickarski (9)
St John's RC School, Bath

VIKING POEM

Vicious and fierce are these people
They wear weird, horned hats
Sailing down streams they go
In seas also.
Their boats with carved animals heads
Can you guess who these people are?
The Vikings of course!

Douglas Kelly (9)
St John's RC School, Bath

MY COUSIN LENNOX

My cousin Lennox
Is funny and cool
He watches Thunderbirds
He plays bombers in the pool.

He likes making maps,
He likes drawing too,
He likes reading with me,
He likes going to the zoo.

He drinks hot chocolate,
He likes eating chips,
He is clever and fun,
He is full of brainy wits.

Caroline Beaverstock (10)
St John's RC School, Bath

MARIA

I am pink,
Bouncy and funny.
I am random weather,
Changing my moods.
I'm a rainbow clock in the wind,
Running and jumping.
A blue tit,
Chatting on.
A bowl of ice cream
Rolling in balls.
I'm me, just me!

Maria Sobey (10)
St John's RC School, Bath

MY KITTEN, MOUSE AND POPPY MY PUPPY

We called her Mouse because she was
Like a little grey ball of fluff
She wasn't always a sweet little thing
But the sight of Poppy was enough.

At first Poppy was treated like dirt
Because she was trying to tease little Mouse
But when she wouldn't be bothered to fight
We welcomed her back into the house.

Now Poppy really isn't a bad little thing
And I love them both as much
But if you try and do as we did
You might not get luck as such.

Wilfred Scolding (10)
St John's RC School, Bath

MY OWN WORLD

My own world would be with
No fighting, no killing,
No suffering or pain,
Everybody living in harmony
People respecting animals.

My own world would be with
No more pollution or acid rain
Everybody looking after the world
No more trees to be cut down

If only that would happen.

James Coram (11)
St John's RC School, Bath

MY FRIEND JAMES

My friend is as tall as a giraffe growing through the clouds.

My friend is as fast as a cheetah with a jet pack.

My friend is as happy as a flower in spring.

My friend is as strong as a lion with a six pack.

My friend is as slow as a snail climbing a mountain.

My friend is as thin as a stick insect on a fruit diet.

My friend is as funny as a monkey with no brain.

My friend is as cool as an ice cub in the North Pole.

My friend is as naughty as me and Zac on a bad day.

My friend is as small as an ant shrinking.

Harry Clesham (8)
St John's RC School, Bath

MY FRIEND

My friend is as fast as a jet packed lightning bolt.
My friend is as strong as a rhinoceros with a sword and some armour.
My friend is as angry as my dad on a bad hair day.
He is as naughty as Dennis the Menace aiming a sling at his dad's head.
He is as sneaky as a spy with invisibility.
He is as nasty as Nasher with the gold medal for being nasty.
He is so good at faking that he will put mud on his own leg to say
                                  someone has kicked him.

Toby Dyson (8)
St John's RC School, Bath

THE ELEARK

The Eleark is half elephant, half shark.

The Eleark is as playful as a toddler in a pool with a chocolate bun
In his hand and a gigantic toy in the other.

The Eleark is as chubby as King Henry VIII
Just eaten a fifteen course meal plus seven puddings.

The Eleark is as noisy as a band with five elephants, ten drums,
Twelve guitars and twenty-five gorillas.

The Eleark is as stinky as five dustbins with smelly socks, rotten fish
And eleven skunks.

The Eleark is as heavy as a herd of elephants having eaten a banquet.

Claudia Emery (8)
St John's RC School, Bath

FRIENDSHIP

Friendship is when you've got a best friend that you can count on.
Friendship is when your friend knows how you feel when you are upset.
Friends are the best present that you can ever get.
They can be the best thing ever
And I know my friends won't let me down.
They are always there for you and I will care for them.
Friendship is someone who knows all about you and tells all your
secrets.

And that's what friendship means to me.

Carol-Anne Shoemark (10)
St John's RC School, Bath

HENRY THE EIGHTH

Henry was a big fat king
Because he ate everything
He was always shouting 'Off with their head'
And after that their blood dripped red.
Wives he had six
What happened to them was a mix.

Catherine of Aragon was his first
But her fate was not the worst.
Anne Boleyn was next in line
Her head was cut off in no time.
Jane Seymour was the one he loved best
She died naturally, unlike some of the rest.

Anne of Cleeves was Henry's fourth wife
She did cause him a lot of strife.
Catherine Howard liked the company of men
Henry didn't like it so headless again.
The last wife was Catherine Parr
She outlived Henry by far.

Michael Prest (9)
St John's RC School, Bath

ROCK AND ROLL

Rock and rollin's here to stay
It will not fade away.
It was meant to be that way
No I don't know why
It just won't die.
I don't care what people say
It just won't fade away.

Jack Baker (11)
St John's RC School, Bath

MUM'S BAD DAY

The birds singing in the sky
Watching mum passing by.
'Mum come quick! I heard Larry say he's been sick!'
'Oh dear this is all I need
When I've got six hungry children to now feed.
OK Larry try not to panic
Although this mess is going to be manic!'
'Mummy, Mummy I've hurt my knee
While I was climbing up that tree.'
'Oh Sarah you silly girl
Can't you see I'm already in a whirl?'
'David and Peter stop messing with my cup of tea
Although I won't have time to drink it as you can see!
Now everyone stop annoying me
Anna's just been stung by a buzzing bee
Now you! Go and fetch me a sick bowl,
Two plasters and Sarah's warm vest
Then please just give me some time to rest!'

Sian Hancock (10)
St John's RC School, Bath

THE LION

As the lion gets ready
To pounce on the deer
It lies still camouflaged in the field
Crawling along the ground
The deer is not aware of the danger it is in
Chewing the grass it knows nothing
It looks up and sees the lion
And runs away in fear.

Bethanie Locke (9)
St John's RC School, Bath

THE BEAUTIFUL WIND

The gentle wind blowing and rushing around me.
The wind twists and twirls brushing up all the leaves in its path.
The wind is swooping and twisting and whirling in every direction.
The wind blowing my hair.
The wind making my umbrella turn inside out.
The forceful wind.
The powerful wind.
The calmful wind.
The peaceful wind.
The harmless wind.
The gentle wind.
The beautiful, breezy wind.

Sophie Weston (10)
St John's RC School, Bath

DRAGON

Silently, the wind sweeps.
No sign of life about
But only dragon seeks space,
When finally it's found a resting place
It shifts its head from side to side
To look for prey to catch.
Then it saw prey and its teeth shined
In the moonlight.
Then it glided into the sky
Watching the prey with his eye
Then down it darted, quick as a bullet
And there the prey lay.

Nathaniel Cross (9)
St John's RC School, Bath

MY FRIEND

My friend is as loud as a baby having an injection.
My friend is as small as a mouse holding a gigantic back pack.
My friend is as angry as a bull when he can't play his Nintendo 64.
My friend is as heavy as Henry VIII.
My friend is as fast as Stephanie Cook.
My friend is as funny as Mr Wilmot.
My friend is as hungry as an ant trapped in a hole for days.
My friend is as skinny as a stick insect on a diet.
My friend is as mad as Mr Blobby on a good day.
My friend is as hot as a deep fat fried chip baked in the sun.
My friend is as fierce as a cheetah holding up its prey.
My friend's hair is as spiky as a hedgehog.
My friend's arms are longer than a snooker cue.
My friend's head is like a bowling ball.
My friend is as clever as J K Rowling
And best of all he will always be my mate!

George Hancock (8)
St John's RC School, Bath

TEACHERS

Teachers are smart, good at art
They are especially picked to be particularly strict.
Have you ever wondered what teachers do at play time?
Do they ring the church bells and go ding dong
Or do they just play ping pong?
What do teachers eat for lunch?
Do they eat green eggs and ham
Or do they eat creamed legs and lamb?
I've seen some old teachers
But do you think there's some bald teachers out there?

Victoria Dent (8)
St John's RC School, Bath

MY FRIEND

My friend is as cold as an ice cube in a can of coke.
My friend is as hairy as a chimpanzee in the zoo.
My friend is as old as a granny in her knitting chair.
My friend is as sweet as a cherry on the top of a cake.
My friend is as daft as Dennis the Menace in the park.
My friend is as slow as a snail with his brakes on
                                    and stuck with super glue.
My friend is as scary as a ghost house.
My friend is as smelly as a skunk.
My friend is so cool that she doesn't have to go to school.
My friend is as noisy as a class of school kids shouting together.

My friend is the best friend in the world.

Phoebe Hall (8)
St John's RC School, Bath

THE DRAGON

The dragon is as hushed as a black panther.
Her breath is as cold as ice.
Her heart is as cold as stone
And her claws are as sharp as the blade of a knife.

Her look is as bitter as icy water.
Her tail is as swift as a feather.
Her teeth sting like a nettle
And her intelligence is stronger than mans.
So beware of the dragon.

Jessica Warlow (10)
St John's RC School, Bath

NIGHT DRAGON

The light of day is now behind
And the moon creeps in my mind.
A dragon prowls upon my thoughts
Smoke curling from his nostrils
Green, smooth scales glisten
Reflected in my thoughts
A looping tail winds round my mind encircling in the dark
Delicate, papery wings flap gently through the night
The light comes creeping in to banish the lonely dragon
But tonight he will return, return will that lonely dragon.

Rachel Prest (10)
St John's RC School, Bath

FLOWERS

Flowers bright, flowers blue, flowers just for me and you.

Poppies swaying in the field
Where war began the territory of man.

Roses red, stand for love
Just the same as up above.

Felicity Perkins (11)
St John's RC School, Bath

WHEN I GO TO SPAIN

When I go to Spain I like the sandy beaches
I love swimming in the sparkling sea
It's hot and loud
When I go shopping in Spain it's crowded
So I went to a café and had a cold drink.

Mary-Jo Book (8)
St John's RC School, Bath

OPHELIA

A beautiful figure of a woman
Floating above the glittering river
Her golden hair floats over her silky gown
Flowers surrounding her body
The sun shining on her silky gown
Her true love does not know where she is
Looking far and wide
Upon this day her true love
Weeps in sorrow
He will never forget his love,
Until he meets in death.

Cassandra Moll (9)
St John's RC School, Bath

TV

I love my TV so much it's funky and it's cool
You really got to watch it now or else you might drool.
Turn on your TV watch it really quick
Or else your mum might turn it off and make you very sick.
You can play your games on it, don't make it very long
Or else your dad might want a go while he sings a song.

Nick Morgan
St John's RC School, Bath

MAY'S WARMTH

May is a warm month
It throws away the coldness
Until there's no more.

Bruce Coram (8)
St John's RC School, Bath

HIGH FLIGHTS

Flying high up in the sky
I could not see any bird or eagle
Flying high up in the sky
All I could see was white
Except for a black dot just below me
I thought at first it was a plane
I lowered down
I saw it was only a blackbird
Flying high as I have ever seen
In my whole life.

Frankie Stratton (9)
St John's RC School, Bath

ALANA

I'm lime green.
I'm a playful kitten.
I'm a summer dress.
I'm The Price Is Right.
I'm fish and chips.
I like to be by the sea
And a very soggy swimming costume.

Alana King (10)
St John's RC School, Bath

ALL QUIET

It is snowing hard
The animals are asleep
And the food is scarce.

Hannah Walsh (8)
St John's RC School, Bath

LIFE AT WAR

Life at war is to feel like a loud firework
Life at war is to hear at home if you survive the war
                                    and you hear bombs in your head.
Life is to feel like you are at war shooting.
Life is to be able to hope that you will still be alive.
Life is to the simple boom in your head
Poppies may save some of these families.
May your heart affect some of these people.

Josie Chandler (9)
St John's RC School, Bath

OPHELIA

Ophelia was so beautiful and wise
With her long, blonde flowing hair
The water so calm with her
The sequins on her dress were slowly slipping off.
She looked very peaceful with her long colourful dress
She was like a golden princess
Going along, the water carrying her
Then she slowly drowned in the clear water.

Sophie West (10)
St John's RC School, Bath

JANUARY

Frosty ice on cars
Thick scarves are worn to keep warm
It is freezing cold.

Jack Griffiths (9)
St John's RC School, Bath

MY FRIEND IS A MONSTER

My friend is as fat as a whale
She's as slow as a snail
She's not funny
Don't pay her any money
But she's as clever as a dog that can talk
And she squawks at me like a hawk
She thinks she's good at football
But I can't see it at all.
She thinks she can make a salad
Whilst listening to a rock ballad
My friend is a monster and everyone knows that . . .

Natalia Rozario (8)
St John's RC School, Bath

PEACE

Peace is a sad and lonely ghost
Walking in the poppy's fields
The war has ended, the war has stopped.

The poppies are growing around the dead soldiers
The earth is filled with tears from people's eyes.

Peace is like a long, long field of poppies.

Ria Harding (10)
St John's RC School, Bath

FUN IN THE WINTER

In the wintertime
It's very cold and frosty
I always have fun.

Adam Arscott (8)
St John's RC School, Bath

THE SEASONS

Spring is when the small birds sing
A mother duck and six ducklings.

Summer's when the sun just pops
And everything is really hot.

Autumn's when the colours show
Green and red and orange glow.

Winter's when the bears go cover
Under the cold snow's powder.

Chrissy Forestell (8)
St John's RC School, Bath

SOPHIE

I am hot pink.
I am a clumsy kitten.
I am an exquisite rainbow.
I am a silky scarf.
I am a warm duvet.
I am Neighbours.
I am a sizzling sausage.
I am me!

Sophie Davies (11)
St John's RC School, Bath

THE MEASLES

I've got the measles
And it isn't very nice.
I've got the measles
And all I eat is ice.

I've got the measles
And they won't go away.
I've got the measles
So come another day.

William Clark (10)
St John's RC School, Bath

THE VOYAGE OF THE RIVER

The voyage of the river
Runs within the bows
Reflecting colours from the pebbles on the ground
Moving silently with only a silent sound
The voyage of the river
The voyage of the river slowly meets the sea
The waves dancing in the gusty breeze
Swooping up the crinkled leaves
The voyage of the river.

Catharine Partridge (10)
St John's RC School, Bath

PAINTS

Paint on my fingers and on my toes,
Paint on my sister, paint on my nose,
Paint on the grass to make it green,
Paint on the walls to make them gleam,
Paint on the bath to make it all glitzy and blue,
Paint on my chocolate just for my mummy and you,
Paint on my cheeks nice and blotchy,
Paint on my fingers, paint on my head, paint on my knees instead!

Natasha Hunt (9)
St John's RC School, Bath

MY FRIEND

M y friend is one of the best
Y ou ought to know that.

F riendly she is
R eady to go
I s that so
E arly up
N ever late
D irty we are never.

Shannon Farrell (9)
St John's RC School, Bath

MOVE . . . FASTER . . .

Snail . . . snail . . . move . . . faster . . .
Your . . . slowness . . . will . . .
End . . . in . . . a . . . disaster . . .
Mrs . . . Blackbird's . . . on . . . your . . .
Trail . . . please . . . go . . . faster . . .
Little . . . snail.

Isabelle Cundy (8)
St John's RC School, Bath

MY FRIEND

My friend is as fast as a cheetah with a rocket,
My friend is as good as wise.

My friend is as funny as a cat chasing its tail
My friend is as good as anyone else.

Ryan Farrell (9)
St John's RC School, Bath

THE CHEESYSAURUS

He is as weak as the world's smallest asthmatic ant trying to pull a lorry
with its handbrake on and ten bags of shopping up a mountain.

He is as smelly as a skunk that has not had a bath since 1485 and has
just eaten a load of garlic he found in a sewage pipe.

He is as unusual as a green alien in a pink swimming pool in a blue
world in a yellow universe.

He is as overweight as an overweight elephant who has just eaten a
celebration bag of high fat peanuts for breaking the record for the
most overweight elephant since the world began.

He is as cold as an icicle in the Ice Age buried in the bottom shelf of an
ice-filled freezer.

He is as a colourful as a very colourful rainbow on a very colourful day
in the Land of Colour.

He is as old as a very old person who thinks that Queen Victoria is still
on the throne.

He is as rich as Bill Gates would be if he won the rollover in
the National Lottery three times in a row.

He is as hairy as a gorilla that has not shaved for a year.

Sylvia Bevan (8)
St John's RC School, Bath

JANUARY

The bright, gleaming sky
As powerful as can be
And a gentle breeze.

Peter Bale (8)
St John's RC School, Bath

JUNE

June starts summer well
Radiant beams from the sun
Will it get hotter?

Edward Hodgkinson (8)
St John's RC School, Bath

DECEMBER

White, glistening frost
The freezing, cold snow crunching
Shining on the ground.

Jack Watson (8)
St John's RC School, Bath

IN FALL

In autumn leaves fall
They grow again in springtime
October's the month.

Tamlyn Tucker (9)
St John's RC School, Bath

AUTUMN

Autumn has now come
All the swallows are going
We are getting cold.

Camilla Patel (8)
St John's RC School, Bath

MY CAT

My cat is a funny thing,
He can't make up his mind if he wants to go out,
Or come in.
He never wants what you give him,
If you put him in his basket he'd rather sleep on a chair,
If you give him water he'll cry,
'Meow I'd rather have milk, it's not fair!'

He may be old but he acts like a kitten,
Running up and down the stairs like a cheetah
Catching his prey,
But then he gets puffed out,
And sleeps for the rest of the day.

With his battered ears and his two-toned nose,
His gleaming eyes and his swishing tail,
His slinky black and white fur and his paws like mittens,
Who could not like him?
I know I can't resist,
He's the best cat in the world, he's my cat Gus!

Sophie Hayes (11)
St Mary's Primary School, Bridgewater

THE MONSTER

This is not a myth
It is a 30ft tall lobster
As it has a gigantic width
Everyone has feelings . . .This is a monster!

People tried to beat it
But the monster just munched them away
And it squashed them with his large, heavy foot,
Not even a bit!
Leaving humans with a pretty tragic day!

All they could do is to avoid it
Having nobody killing this creature
No one felt that this monster was a twit,
People to the monster were litter!

Nevertheless, one day it came!
The making of large detonators were completed
Which meant people were not even making it tame
At last, this killer has been defeated!

Adnan Haq (11)
St Mary's Primary School, Bridgewater

THE WORLD'S A FUNNY PLACE

The world is a funny place,
But I'm lucky to be in it,
Most people don't get what they want,
But for me, the world is enough.

Why must everyone fight?
Why must we all quarrel?
It really gets on my nerves,
I'm soon going to explode.

I feel incredibly bored,
And very annoyed,
I seriously need a life,
Why can't I be free?

Music is the only air I breathe,
Bars are all I ever see,
The world is a funny place,
I've never even seen the sea.

Edward Scarratt (11)
St Mary's Primary School, Bridgewater

MY CAT

My cat Thomas is black as velvet,
He has sharp teeth as white as a sheep,
And he moves as slowly as a dark night.
He purrs like an engine starting,
He's as fierce as a stormy night,
And he eats as fast as a cheetah runs.

He's fun when he's not being grumpy like an elephant,
And he's cute and smooth like a teddy bear
That's why I love my cat Thomas.

Naomi Gibbs (10)
St Mary's Primary School, Bridgewater

SNOW

As autumn leaves the sky
Snow falls, crispy and white with all its might
As spring takes over
Winter starts to cry.

Max Jaydee Spenn (8)
St Paul's School, Shepton Mallet

WIND

Wind is blowing,
Tornadoes are hurling,
Dogs are barking,
Cats are miaowing,
They want to be safe and sound.

Wind is blowing,
People are whizzed around,
Kids are yelling, mums are crying,
They aren't safe and sound.

But suddenly . . .

Francesca Bean
St Paul's School, Shepton Mallet

SNOW!

As the autumn leaves the sky
Winter takes its place,
Bushes covered in a thick layer,
Cars can't stand it any more,
Dogs and children shiver with joy,
The time has come for the sun to appear.
Tears come,
Watch it melt,
Remember the good times,
It will be back for fun once more.

Natalie Brown (9)
St Paul's School, Shepton Mallet

HORSE POEM

It's a graceful galloper,
Hay eater,
People carrier,
Carriage puller,
Tail swayer,
Noisy neigher,
Race winner,
Mischief maker,
High jumper,
Baby breeder,
Grass cruncher,
Muddy roller,
Saddle wearer,
Fast trotter,
Water survivor,
Quick canterer,
Hard worker,
Strong kicker,
And a toe hurter,
    H o r s e!

Georgina Baker (9)
St Paul's School, Shepton Mallet

RABBITS

Hopping mad
Jumping dad
Munching proudly
Sleeping loudly
Sniffing sadly
Hunting gladly

Zoe Lianne Thick (8)
St Paul's School, Shepton Mallet

MONKEYS

Tree shaker,
Nit pickers,
Branch hanger,
Sweet lovers,
Lovely cuddlers,
Banana eaters,
Car chasers,
Finger sucker,
People watcher,
Mad runner,
Cool jumper,
Night sleeper,
Game players,
Leaf breaker
    That's monkeys for you!

Louise Taylor (9)
St Paul's School, Shepton Mallet

DOGS

When they run fast
Their ears will flap,
When they get tired
They sit on your lap
All through the night
They tickle your toes
And say they love you
By licking your nose!

Lauren Becky Short (8)
St Paul's School, Shepton Mallet

RAINBOW

As green as grass
As blue as the sky
As red as roses
As purple as a chocolate wrapper
As yellow as the sun
As black as night
As white as paper
As pink as a flower
As gold as treasure
As orange as an orange
As silver as a seat
As brown as wood.

Adam Kirby (8)
St Paul's School, Shepton Mallet

SNAKE

Slithery slimer
Wrap trapper
Sneaky creeper
Hole napper
Wriggly slider
Mouse catcher
Red sneaker
S n a k e!

Dean Roles (8)
St Paul's School, Shepton Mallet

RABBITS

Long eared furball,
Carrot cruncher,
Fence leaper,
Tail thumper,
Nose twitcher,
Tongue tingler,
Teeth grinder,
Hay snuggler,
High hopper,
Quick runner.
    R a b b i t s!

Aimee Chinnock (9)
St Paul's School, Shepton Mallet

DOLPHINS

Loud squealer,
Fish eater,
Tail wagger,
Water splasher,
Graceful swimmer,
Sloppy player,
Lovely twirler,
Deep diver,
    Lovely Dolphins!

Vicky Brice (9)
St Paul's School, Shepton Mallet

SEALS

Penguin pouncer
Cod catcher
Super swimmer
Grey glistener
Flipper flapper
Seal squisher
Baby breeder
Fish fetcher
Furry slider
Slippery squeaker.

Abby James (8)
St Paul's School, Shepton Mallet

GORILLA

Tree shaker
Noise maker
Fast runner
Chest banger
Bad tempered
Good hider
Fast swinger
Funny shouter
          Gorilla!

Ross Catley (8)
St Paul's School, Shepton Mallet

SNOW!

Fun spiller
Shiver giver
Path filler
Snowball stinger
Excitement singer
As the autumn leaves the sky,
Winter takes a place in one's eye.

Stephanie Lamb (8)
St Paul's School, Shepton Mallet

CRABS

Leg pincher
Slow walker
Six legger
Little eater
Side walker
Sound scuttler
Deep burier.

Stacey Louise Horler (8)
St Paul's School, Shepton Mallet

CHAMELEON

Colour changer
Googley eyer
Slow mover
Gun tonguer
Sticky footer
Chameleon.

Thomas McClure (9)
St Paul's School, Shepton Mallet

SNOW

Slippery slidey all over the place
It tastes cold shimmers like gold
Wrap up, it's freezing, the wind is breezing.
Cold in your face to play with, it's ace
As the autumn cries away
It will come another day
Slippery slidey all over the place.

Callum Otter (8)
St Paul's School, Shepton Mallet

WIND

Roughy and toughy it batters the trees
Swiftly and smoothly through my knees
Quickly and easily in the air
Rustly and bustly in my hair
Briskly and wildly it goes so near
Eating and beating it hurts my ear
W i n d!

Thomas Pennyfather (9)
St Paul's School, Shepton Mallet

OUR SCHOOL

Monday rains pouring drops
Tuesday girls wear skirts and tops
Wednesday sunshine gleaming bright
Thursday rains day and night
Friday brings joy for schools
Saturday happiness for St Pauls.

Elouise Whittaker (8)
St Paul's School, Shepton Mallet

GUESS THE ANIMAL

It's a prey scarer,
Spotty runner,
Prey hunter,
Branch snatcher,
Prey catcher,
Jungle jumper,
Prey eater,
      it's a
            L e o p a r d!

Jamie Willmott (8)
St Paul's School, Shepton Mallet

SNAKE

Tail rattler
Human eater
Rat trapper
Sneaky peeker
Slim creature
Fast striker
Green slimer
It's only a
S n a k e!

Jamie Hunt (8)
St Paul's School, Shepton Mallet

BAD THINGS ABOUT DOGS

Headache giver
Fur clinger
Mud leaver
Furniture chewer
Noisy bather
Bum biter
Oh, why did we buy this thing, *a dog!*

Charlete Alice Claydon (9)
St Paul's School, Shepton Mallet

HORSE

Fence jumper
Race winner
Fast galloper
Tail swisher
Pooh plopper
Hay eater
    H o r s e!

George Alex Wolff (8)
St Paul's School, Shepton Mallet

BALLET

I like to wear my tutu, it's lilac
I like to wear my shoes
They are pink
I like to bounce around and sing
I do lots of shows in the Town Hall
Ballet is my thing.

Carla Jane Lambert (7)
Sedgemoor Manor Junior School

ESCAPADES

I have no luck with pets . . .
I had a fish
But it swam,
I had a cat
But it purred away,
I had a bee
But it buzzed off,
And my stick insect but it wouldn't stick around,
I had a deer
But it wouldn't come near,
I had a spider
But it wouldn't stay either,
I had a frog
But it leaped away,
And my antelope
. . . eloped
I had a duck,
But it waddled away,
Even my slug wouldn't stay,
My little bird,
Flew away home,
And my moose
. . . vamoosed,
My owl one day just flew,
My badger
Ran away,
My seagull
Went home,
My kangaroo

Took a homeward bound,
Even my sloth wouldn't hang around,
So now I've decided,
No more pets for me,
Pets are too much bother,
If I want a smelly creature
Round the house,
I'll settle for my baby brother.

Catherine Ann Baker (10)
Sedgemoor Manor Junior School

LIFE'S BEEN GREAT IN MY FAMILY

Life's been great in my family,
Since the day my family won the Lottery
My parents brought a new sports car
And lots of fine pottery

I have lots of new clothes,
I'm running up the wall
My mum and dad aren't fighting
Instead they're at the mall.

I have lots of cool friends,
I'm always hangin' out
My mum doesn't know where I am
And my grandad always shouts.

We have lots of slaves,
They do all the work
My sister is always jealous
And she likes to lurk about.

Chloe Simmonds (11)
Sedgemoor Manor Junior School

School Poem!

School is cool
School is great
School is what we celebrate
Art, maths and so much more
Dancing in the sun with glory
School is fun
At this school you can run
You can giggle
And glee and laugh with me
School is crazy
School is calm
School is what we do with harm
School is funny
It's just like honey
School is what we like to do
And it will always be with you!

Jasmine Lewis (8)
Sedgemoor Manor Junior School

Family

My name is Stacey Heard
I have a family of four
Mum
Dad
Brother
And me
We are not rich or poor
I have a cat called Smokey
She is very friendly
These are the people that
Make my family.

Stacey Heard (10)
Sedgemoor Manor Junior School

THE LIFE OF MATT

There was a boy called Matt
He had hair as red as a cat
Whenever he spoke
Or yawned he choked
And that was in the Army.

There was a man called Matt
He died his hair as blue as a bat
When he got home
His wife said 'Ahhhhhh!'
And that was the end of that.

There was an OAP called Matt
He had hair as grey as a gnat
He died
And all he left was his cat
And that was the life of Matt.

Daniel Gooding (10)
Sedgemoor Manor Junior School

I AM

I am what I'm good at
I am what I play
I am what I'm feeling
I am what I say
I am what I look like
I am what I do
I am what I am inside
I am thinking of you.

Who am I?

Sam Godfrey (10)
Sedgemoor Manor Junior School

I HAVE NO LUCK WITH PETS (ESCAPADES)

I have no luck with pets . . .
I had a cat
But he paused away,
I had a budgie
But it budged off,
I had a fish
But he bubbled it,
And my stick insect
Wouldn't stick around.

I had an elephant
But she blew it,
I had a zebra
But it camouflaged,
I had a tiger
But it striped off,
And my antelope . . . eloped.

I had a duck
But it waddled away,
But even my hare sped away
My round potato bug
Flew away home,
And my moose
. . . vamoosed.

My ants fled
My bamboo climbed high,
My mouse squeaked off,
My kangaroo took a homeward bound,

Even my sloth wouldn't hang around,
So now I decided
No more pets for me
Pets are too much bother
If I want a smelly creature
Around the house
I'll settle for my baby brother.

Victoria Puk (110
Sedgemoor Manor Junior School

MY HATES AND LIKES

Footballers have matches on it
Broken glass is found on it
Grass
I like that stuff.

You play ice hockey on it
You can trip and break your leg on it
Ice
I hate that stuff.

You can throw it at people
You can make snowmen with it
Snow
I like that stuff.

You can shoot it at people
The army use them
Guns and bullets
I hate them.

Karl Cowlin (10)
Sedgemoor Manor Junior School

ESCAPADES

I have no luck with pets . . .
I had a hippopotamus
But he muddled away
I had a dolphin
But it somersaulted off
I had a bird
But he flapped it
And my stick insect
Wouldn't stick around.
I had a hamster
But she chewed away
I had a dog
But it barked off
I had a goat
But it butted away
And my antelope . . .
Eloped.
I had an elephant
But it stomped off
Even my alligator
Snapped away
My moth
Flew away home
And my moose . . .
. . . vamoosed.
My horse hoofed it
My unicorn wished away
My maggots ate away
My kangaroo took a homeward bound
Even my sloth wouldn't hang around.

So now I've decided
No more pets for me
Pets are too much bother.
If I want a smelly creature
Around the house
I'll settle for my baby brother.

Danielle Mansfield
Sedgemoor Manor Junior School

THE MOON AND SUN

The sun is a golden toilet seat
The moon is a bright white toilet seat
The sun is a golden vase
The sun is golden animals
The moon is a white vase
The moon is bright white animals
Our teachers are the sun and the moon
Your mums are the sun and the moon
The sun is a golden TV
The moon is a bright white TV.

Luke Cannard (8)
Sedgemoor Manor Junior School

UP, UP AND AWAY

Up, up and away like an aeroplane,
Up, up and away I like to play a game
Up, up and away I like to sing a song
Up, up and away it's a nice day today.

Cassandra Gilliard (9)
Sedgemoor Manor Junior School

MY FAVOURITE THINGS

My favourite TV programme is Sabrina The Teenage Witch
My favourite colour is purple
My favourite pet is my dog
My favourite pop group is S Club 7
My favourite video is Stuart Little
My favourite type of car is a soft top
My favourite object is everything
My favourite animal is a dog
My favourite song by S Club 7 is 'Never Had A Dream Come True'
My favourite friend is Sarah Edwards
My favourite type of flower is a sunflower
My favourite type of clothing is trousers.

Abby Mitchell (7)
Sedgemoor Manor Junior School

MY FEELINGS

M   y feelings are emotional and private
Y   ou should hardly ever have unhappy feelings.

F   eelings are nice most of the time.
E   motional feelings make people happy
E   veryone has feelings for someone special
L   ove is a very good feeling
I   nside your heart you have feelings
N   ice people, nice feelings
G   ood days, good feelings
S   ad is very emotional and unhappy.

Rachel Harvey (10)
Sedgemoor Manor Junior School

ESCAPADES

I have no luck with pets . . .
I had a koala
But he climbed away
I had a wasp
But he buzzed off
I had a bird
But he fluttered away
And my stick insect
Wouldn't stick around
Then . . .
I had a rabbit
But she hopped along her way
I had a fish
But he was taken away for the main dish of the day
I had a dog
But he ate a log
And my Antelope
Eloped
And finally . . .
I had a caterpillar
But he wriggled away
Even my snake went off and married a
Girl called Kay.
Now I know . . .
I have no luck with animals at all!

Hope Evans (11)
Sedgemoor Manor Junior School

LIFE'S BEEN GREAT IN MY FAMILY

Life's been great in my family
Since the day that my new puppy came,
I really adore her and
She really adores me.

I get all the attention
But she looks sad,
She knows I really love her
I love her like mad.

I think she's an angel
My mum thinks she's a prune
I think she's cuddly
And prune.

She keeps me warm on a cold chilly night
She comes under my covers ooh what a sight
She looks like my young cute brothers.

Rachel Lawrence (11)
Sedgemoor Manor Junior School

FAT TONY

F   at Tony quick run they say
A   s he comes
T   hey all think he's mean some even say he's the Chaos King.

T   he big mean machine if
O   nly he would be kind
N   o I can't change Fat Tony
Y   ou should not grow up like him.

Michael Cannard (10)
Sedgemoor Manor Junior School

LIFE'S BEEN GREAT IN MY FAMILY

Life's been great in my family,
Since the day the elephant came,
She sleeps in the barn at night,
What a wonderful sight.

We both get all the attention,
'I bought that elephant,' my mum always mentions
I have to go and get her food,
But I haven't got any money and mum's in a mood.

She takes me for long and short rides,
Whatever she decides,
She wakes me up in the morning but that's OK
So I go and get her some hay.

She's grey she's cute she's cuddly,
But now she's all muddy,
Oh no not again
She's gone and eaten up her reins.

Nicole Hill (10)
Sedgemoor Manor Junior School

MY OLD FRIEND JAKE

My old friend Jake
Was as thin as a snake
Light as a drop of rain
One windy day
Jake blew away
And was never seen again.

Shaun Whitcombe & Chris Power (10)
Sedgemoor Manor Junior School

ESCAPADES

I have no luck with pets . . .
I had a cat
But he pawed away

I had an alligator
But it snapped off
I had an elephant
But he stomped away

And my stick insect
Wouldn't stick around!
I had some ants
But they marched back to the army

I had a pig
But it plodded off
and my antelope . . .
. . . eloped

I had a spider
But it legged it
My kangaroo
Took a homeward bound
Even my sloth
Wouldn't hang around

So now I've decided
No more pets for me
Pets are too much bother
If I want a smelly creature
Round the house
I'll settle for my baby brother.

Jodie Millar (11)
Sedgemoor Manor Junior School

WHO AM I?

I am what I drink
I am what I say
I am what I move
I am what I think
I am what I write
I am what I touch
I am what I learn
I am what I rip
I am what I look at
I am what I plant
I am what I throw
I am what I blow
I am what I throw away
I am what I kick
I am what I sing
I am what I play
I am what I am.

Ian Fuller (10)
Sedgemoor Manor Junior School

PETS POEM

Pets are big
Pets are small
Pets take a lot of care
At least a bit after school
But not on the landing
Or in the hall.

Tara Steel (10)
Sedgemoor Manor Junior School

MY FRIEND CARLA LAMBERT ABOUT FRUIT

My friend eats bananas
Puts them in her pyjamas
Carla's such a giggle
When she has a tickle
When she puts bananas in her lamp
She gets such a cramp
When she sees a person she goes and curses them.

And when she makes a pear
She goes over there
Then she sees another pear
But doesn't really care
You lovely pear
While you go over there
I will go and share.

Stacie Burton (7)
Sedgemoor Manor Junior School

SCHOOL TIME

School is cool
Cause no one drools
Having lots of friends
Oh! When they defend
Oh what nice work the teachers say
Loading the computers but they don't have time to play.

Time for play the bell says
Ice is outside and everyone has a good play
Mum says had a good day
Even though I like school
Sometimes it can be a bit of a pay day.

Kim Lewin (9)
Sedgemoor Manor Junior School

SPRING

Flowers grow
Lambs are born
Blossom on the tree

Children laughing
Having fun
Birds are singing joyfully

Hedgehogs and tortoises
Came out from their sleep
Out of their beds their noses peep

The sun comes out
Bright and early
Shining on the earth below.

Kirsty Newman (10)
Sedgemoor Manor Junior School

SNOW

Snow, snow, snow is white
Snow is falling in the night
Wake in the morning and it's so bright
Children out playing in the snow
All nice and warm with the Ready Brek glow.

Jade Smith (10)
Sedgemoor Manor Junior School

MY DOG

My dog has pinched my sock
He has run off round the block.
When I called him
He came to me
But he'd been naughty, so got no tea!

Megan Lewin (7)
Sedgemoor Manor Junior School

HAMSTERS ARE

Hamsters are cute
Hamsters are cuddly
Hamsters are sweet
Hamsters are so loveable don't you agree?

Hayleigh Bryant (10)
Sedgemoor Manor Junior School

THE SPOOK

I get it every year on Hallowe'en,
I don't know how to stop it.
My friends just say I'm mental,
But I just say I'm not.

They say 'Don't be stupid,'
I tell them 'It's true!'
They don't understand me,
Do you?

I am walking home on Hallowe'en night,
And it happens.
At precisely eight o'clock
Dong Dong Dong . . .

The ghosts from all the graveyards,
In front of my eyes.
I try to scream,
But no sound comes out.

This year I'm dreading so much,
Dong Dong Dong . . .
Oh No! It's time,
Here they come.

I have my torch this year,
I shine it in front of me.
Aghhhhhh!
I can scream.

Then I look more closely and say 'Hello,'
They take off their sheets and say 'BOO!'
My school friends! The Spook! What a fool I've been,
Now I love the spook on Hallowe'en!

Melanie Palmer (11)
Wells Cathedral Junior School

OIL SLICK

I was watching the six o'clock news
When something caught my eye!
'Major oil slick
Boat crash on rock,
Split barrels and barrels of oil!'
I jumped when the producer said
There was danger for the animals on the Galapagos Islands!

That night I had nightmares
About the poor animals.
But in the morning I said a prayer for the wind
To carry the oil out to sea
And not towards the islands.

After school the same day
I raced back home to see the news
And it seemed God had answered my prayer.
But there was still a tiny danger
Of the wind changing direction
All I have to do now is keep on praying
And wait . . .

Lauren Longstaff (10)
Wells Cathedral Junior School

DOLPHINS AND BEES

Dolphins live in seas,
They play all day,
Unlike the bees,
Who work on the way.

Dolphins, always friendly,
Never let you down,
Playing endlessly,
Smiling like a clown!

Bees are busy buzzing,
And very stripy too,
If you are annoying,
They might sting you.

Rowena Fellows (10)
Wells Cathedral Junior School

WALES

I love her mountains, her music.
I love her books, her brilliancy.
I love her people, her towns and shopping centres.
I love the silence, the wilderness.

The air, the life, the barren rocks.
The tiny, tumbling tarns on hillside:
Moving, always moving.
The vast, black and grey lakes
Seemingly dead.

The roar of the crowds,
The beeping of horns on the jam-packed streets
In the south.

The dead, but not so dead, calm
In the north.

But all I need is there,
Silence,
Uproar,
Beauty,
People,
Silence!
Wales.

Nicholas Rawlings (10)
Wells Cathedral Junior School

RUNNING AWAY FROM HOME!

On a bright sunny day,
I ran away from home,
I went into the street,
And hid in a yard.

A man walked past and said,
'What are you doing.'
I replied and whispered,
'Who are you.'

He suddenly vanished and I ran on more,
I didn't know where I was,
So I turned round,
And went back to the place I came from.

In the place where the man was,
My dad was there and he shouted,
'Where have you been'
I replied,
'I don't know.'

Then he took me back home
And shouted at me for being late for school!

Rhys Pullin (10)
Wells Cathedral Junior School

CHILDREN

Children play in the forest wild
While the long days run out
May they see the world around
The sun round, young and fresh
The grass sweet smell
The forest dew
Yet not the day that they will play forever.

In Heaven's fold
The Christ child there
The little sunray's gleam
Like crystals whole and pure
Then in the cloud come God's children
Old but still the same
This is where they will play forever.

Minty Buxton (11)
Wells Cathedral Junior School

CRICKET

Every spectator is hushed.
The batsman are tense
To survive that final hour of that last day
Of that last test
In 1942.

Then, out of the silence,
The wailing of the air raid siren
Sang out over Lords.

Suddenly, panic struck.
Everyone was ushered out of the ground
And into the nearest air raid shelter.

The whistling was all too distinct.
The planes had been circling
For over an hour.
This was their first bomb dropped.
And it landed.

Right
In the middle of Lords.

Sam Laing (10)
Wells Cathedral Junior School

CATS

Cats come in different shapes and sizes
Black, grey or white
Ginger and with stripes
They purr when you stroke them
They lie in the sun
They're lazy half the time
Then they want their lunch
Their fur is so soft when you stroke them
Their fur is so warm
They like to play in boxes and with string too
They like to go on windowsills, beds, up trees or in a shed
They like to play with balls and decorations too
They lick their tails and their faces too
They also like to dig their claws in to you
All in all I'll give them a hundred per cent
Cats are the best so praise them
Amen.

Philip Bolton (10)
Wells Cathedral Junior School

HOLIDAY

I love to go far away,
Especially on my holiday.
Just to play there on the beach
And kick a ball right out of reach.

My mother says be careful,
I may not get it back.
When I give that ball,
Such a frightful *whack!*

After that I go to sea.
On my lilo with a cup of tea.
And before we go on home,
I have an ice cream cone.

Joe Corp (10)
Wells Cathedral Junior School

THE OCEAN

Blacks, yellows, greens and blues,
All within the sea,
The gentle waves,
The midnight sky,
As scenic as can be.

The crashing tide overlaps,
The silent nigh awakes.
The sun comes out,
The sea calms down,
The morning makes its break.

The sun is bright and shining,
The air is fresh and light.
There is a cry,
From a seabird,
Which travels through the night.

It lands gently on the sand,
The golden gleaming bed.
It pecks and chews,
And never stops,
To look and lift its head.

Ruby Chan (11)
Wells Cathedral Junior School

THE BIRD'S FLIGHT

As the birds fly
Up high in the sky
And their colour
As the sky gets duller
The feather on a wing
And a note as they sing.

As their wings beat
The birds can eat
From county to county
And country to country
As the birds fly
Up high in the sky

The seasons will go by.

Austin Squibbs (10)
Wells Cathedral Junior School

THE OCEAN

The ocean is deep, magnificent and blue,
Huge and wonderful to see
What would we do without it?
It's a part of life for me.

Cutting and weaving around each little island
The ocean makes its path,
But there is a mystery about this ocean
That can't be revealed in a photograph.

Not a soul knows that mystery
Of the deep ocean blue.

Sarah Balmer (10)
Wells Cathedral Junior School

FEELINGS

My feelings are closed off from me,
My feelings are running away from me;
My feelings feel like porridge, grey and lumpy,
Sometimes my feelings explode
With happiness or even reel with sadness,
Feelings are funny things,
They're like rollercoasters, happy, excited,
Sad, depressed, happy, excited, sad, depressed,
And while I stand alone in this empty place,
My thoughts take me to another place,
Somewhere, away from this dreadful place of sadness,
Away,
Going, going, *gone.*

Tatiana Haigh (11)
Wells Cathedral Junior School

THE SONNET

How shall I write a sonnet it's so hard,
The form of rhyme and rhythm is complex,
My brain is all a whirl like beaten lard,
Thought is not an automatic reflex.
To write a love song really is not cool,
My friends would laugh and mock at my expense.
Perhaps I should be lying by a pool,
And thoughts would flow like water bringing sense.
My dog appears, she stares with loving eyes,
How can I help, you look so lost she whines;
Oh come and play and leave the work she sighs,
When we return I'll help you to write your lines.
I leave my pen and go and have some fun,
When I get back I find the sonnet done!

Alexander Palmer (10)
Wells Cathedral Junior School

THE WARRIOR'S CRY

The young must grow old
As the old grow older,
And cowards will shrink
As the bold grow bolder.
Courage may blossom in quiet hearts
For who can tell where bravery starts;
Truth is a song oft lying unsung
All must hear it for peace to be won.
Those who lay down their lives for friends
Their echo rolls onwards it never ends.
'Til evil arrives, a wicked horde,
Driving a warrior to pick up his sword.
The honourable win straight and fair,
Justice is with us, beware, beware.

William Hatcher (10)
Wells Cathedral Junior School

COLOURS

Red is the colour of sweet, sweet strawberries
Orange is the colour of the burning sun
Yellow is the colour of a bunch of bananas
Green is the colour of my mother's eyes
Blue is the colour of a cloudless sky
Indigo is the colour of a jewellery box
Violet is the colour of a hair band
These are the colours of our world!

Florence Cook (11)
Wells Cathedral Junior School

ELEPHANT FOR SALE

We've an elephant for sale
He's big and grey,
He came from Africa
At least that's what they say.

He has a long trunk
Which makes a loud noise,
He is very fat
And squirts water at boys.

We've had him for years
He's a family pet,
But now he's too big
And so cannot be kept.

We must find a good home
Where he can stay till he dies,
He loves taking baths
And making mud pies.

Please, someone come soon
He just can't stay here,
Our flat is too small
And he drinks all the beer!

So, if you have enough space
And a very large door,
My telephone number
Is 3764.

Lauren Brown (11)
Wells Cathedral Junior School

THE SEASONS

The year has woken
Spring is here
The grass is green
And the sky is clear
The ice will melt
And the rain disappear;

Spring is gone
And the sun's come out
It's summertime without a doubt
The children play in light all day
And the birds all build nests to lay;

Autumn's here
With thunderstorms
The clouds are grey
From dusk to dawn
The plants will die
From weather bound
And the birds will all
Start flying south;

Winter's here
And the trees are white
The houses are covered in blankets delight
The roads are icy
And the fire is on
Christmas is here
And the New Year's rung.

Robert Edmondson (10)
Wells Cathedral Junior School

TREES

A
Fir
Tree.
A big one.
A small one.
Thin ones, fat ones.
Palm trees with big leaves.
Chestnut trees with medium leaves.
Christmas trees with shiny silver bells.
Bare winter trees with snow on branches.
Climbing
Trees, I
Enjoy.
Going up
High. It is fun.
Look how high I am now.

Michael Barnard (11)
Wells Cathedral Junior School

HOBBITS

Hobbits live in holes
Hobbits hate all trolls
Hobbits are very small
Hobbits aren't very cool
Hobbits dig holes in dirt
Hobbits like the name Albert
Hobbits don't wear shoes
Hobbits like to know the news
Hobbits like six meals a day
Hobbits like to play games.

William Newcomb (10)
Woolavington Village Primary School

TEN HAPPY

Ten happy parents,
Went to a little dine
One choked and then there were nine

Nine happy parents,
Went fishing with their bait
One fell in and there were eight.

Eight happy parents,
Went to beautiful Devon
One threw up and then there were seven.

Seven happy parents,
Went to have a fun dive and fix
One fell over and then there were six

Six happy parents,
Met a man called Clive
One married him and then there were five

Five happy parents,
Declared a civil war
One got bombed and then there were four

Four happy parents,
Roamed the country land free
One encountered a bear and then there were three

Three happy parents,
Went to the loo
One got stuck and then there were two

Two happy parents,
Ate a current bun
One ate too many
And then there was one.

One sad parent,
Decided to beat a nun
He got arrested
And then there were none.

Robert Johns (11)
Woolavington Village Primary School

VALENTINE'S DAY

Valentine's Day is a day for lovers,
The girl is still under her covers.
She wakes up to find it's Valentine's Day.
And not the end of May.
Some time she might remember.
Valentine's Day is near December.
She goes out to find her man,
And she goes out to find him in his van
She looks inside she finds her man,
But he says where is your nan?
Next might come the engagement ring,
Then we will hear the church bells ting.
They might come down the aisle a bride and groom,
After dinner they'll go check out their hotel room.
They go to a disco dance with all their heart,
They say to each other they will never be apart.
The girls shall dance all night,
While men are at the pub having a pint.
By the time they get home,
It's gone 2 o'clock and they say 'Oh no!'
Family and friends could never complain,
They celebrate only with Champagne.
This is the end of Valentine's Day,
Single people might shout 'Hip Hip Hooray!'

Hollie Wells (10)
Woolavington Village Primary School

TEN HAPPY NUTTERS

Ten happy nutters went to dine,
One choked on chips
And then there were nine.

Nine happy nutters went on a date,
One was dumped
And then there were eight.

Eight happy nutters went to Devon,
One got lost
And then there were seven.

Seven happy nutters done some tricks
One disappeared
And then there were six.

Six happy nutters went for a dive.
One missed the board
And then there were five.

Five happy nutters knocked on a door,
One was slapped
And then there were four.

Four happy nutters had a bad knee,
One knee cracked
And then there were three.

Three happy nutters went to the loo,
One fell down
And then there were two.

Two happy nutters found a gun,
One shot himself
And then there was one.

One miserable nutter found a shot gun,
He shot his eye
And then there were none!

James Michael Reade (11)
Woolavington Village Primary School

MANCHESTER UNITED

Manchester United are the best
They are better than all the rest
Man U score every single game
They should be in everybody's window frame
David Beckham crosses from the right
Andy Cole always has a fight.

Man U win against Coventry City
The Manager should have moved to a different city
Man U beat Liverpool
Roy Keane is very cool
Ryan Giggs beating the pack
Teddy Sheringham on the attack.

Man U beat Man City
What a pity
The goalkeeper is starting to fade
Everyone gets paid
Ryan Giggs scores a goal
He made a big hole.

Craig Taplin (10)
Woolavington Village Primary School

ANIMALS POEM

I like animals with fluffy wings,
Lions, cheetahs all sorts of things
I have a dog and a cat,
My cat lies by the fire on her hairy mat.

I saw a bear,
With fluffy hair.
A toucan too that started to squawk
As if it wanted to have a talk.

I saw a seal,
Eating a fish meal,
He was playing with a golden ball,
That a princess lost in the oyster pool.

Holly Jago (10)
Woolavington Village Primary School

ICE CREAM

Ice cream is my favourite food,
I mush it up like runny poo.
Then I eat it with a slurp,
After that I do a burp.

My favourite flavour is mint ice cream,
Or it could be strawberry it seems.
When my mum gives it to me,
I look at it like the sea.

My daddy eats it in a chump,
And I only get a little lump.
I love it when I go out,
Because I can always feel my mouth.

Vicky Moore (9)
Woolavington Village Primary School

ALIEN MICE

The alien mice they don't like rice,
But they do like chocolate and cheese,
They like the moon and also Mars,
And they like looking up at the stars.

The Emperor Mouse he lives in a house,
That is very heavily guarded,
His daughter is extremely sad,
After her father says she is bad.

The mice are deep green,
And serve evil masters,
They are very weird,
And they don't grow beards.

Simon Hann (9)
Woolavington Village Primary School

POEM

My mummy is a star,
My daddy makes a bar,
My brother's going to drive a car,
And I eat a Mars bar

My nanny's good at knitting,
My grandad's good at fixing.
My friends are good at listening,
And I'm always missing.

My auntie has long hair,
My uncle is a pair,
My friends care,
And my pony is a mare.

Rebecca Chidgey (8)
Woolavington Village Primary School

MY PONIES

I've got two ponies one fat, one thin,
I've got two ponies one brown, one white
I've got two ponies one tall, one short,
I've got two ponies with a lot of might.

I've got two ponies and they're very fast
I've got two ponies I want them to last
I've got two ponies they are fun
I've got two ponies they're loved by everyone.

I've got two ponies that live in a stable
I've got two ponies and they're not called Mable
I've got two ponies one girl, one boy
I've got two ponies they're full of joy.

I've got two ponies.

Hannah Halliday (10)
Woolavington Village Primary School

CLARE'S HAIR

There was a girl called Clare,
Who just couldn't brush her hair,
She was on the phone,
And blew the loan
And wasn't allowed to the fair.

She said it was unfair,
She went upstairs
When she got to the top,
She was in a strop,
Then she shouted it's not fair.

Gemma Walford (10)
Woolavington Village Primary School

My Family

My mummy loves me very much,
My brother's really mad.
My daddy smokes and drinks too much,
We tell him it's really bad.

My nanny's good at knitting,
My granddad's old and dozey.
My dog is getting very old,
And also very nosey.

My auntie's very caring,
My uncle tries to be funny
My little cousin's only 1,
And always wants his dummy.

Megan Pope (9)
Woolavington Village Primary School

Food And Drink

Food

Food is yummy
Food is scrummy
When you're hungry
You can eat it

Drinks

Drink is lovely
Drink is wuvely
When you're out of breath
You drink it.

Felicity Adkins (8)
Woolavington Village Primary School

WHY DID THE CHILDREN ... ?

Why did the children build a cavity?
When the one thing we told them
Was not to build a cavity.

Why did the children climb into the washing machine?
When the one thing we told them
Was not to climb into the washing machine.

Why did the children drink alcohol?
When the one thing we told them
Was not to drink alcohol.

Why did the children put milk in their hair?
When the one thing we told them
Was not to put milk in their hair.

Why did the children drive a motorbike?
When the one thing we told them
Was not to drive a motorbike.

Steven Vaughan (10)
Woolavington Village Primary School

MONAY THE FOX

In a city far away,
There lived a fox called Monay,
By night she robbed and stealed,
By day she groomed and healed.

For a fox so cute and shy,
Monay was gone in the wink of an eye,
It had been said that she'd been seen
But she's so quick it was probably a dream.

Dean O'Toole (10)
Woolavington Village Primary School

MY PETS

When I come home from school
And walk through the door
I am greeted by my pets
1, 2, 3 and 4

My hamster is called Rachel
She's a perfect darling
But when she gets angry
She starts snarling

My cats are called Rosie and George
They're quite outstanding
When they jump from a great height
They always have a perfect landing

My dog is called Bexley
He's totally daft
But when he gets dirty
He hates having a bath.

Natasha Webber (8)
Woolavington Village Primary School

WHY DID THE . . . ?

Why did the children sow seeds
When the first thing we told them
Was to sow beads.

Why did the children throw dirt
When the first thing we told them
Was to do work.

Why did the children wipe their feet
When the first thing we told them
Was to eat meat.

Kim Moore (11)
Woolavington Village Primary School

IF I HAD WINGS

If I had wings I would fly to the stars,
If I had wings I would land on Mars,
I had wings I would fly around,
If I had wings I wouldn't walk on ground.

If I had wings I would fly up and down,
If I had wings I would float into town,
If I had wings it would be great,
If I had wings it would be like my best mate.

Amy Sparrow (9)
Woolavington Village Primary School

DON'T DO THAT

Don't do,
Don't do,
Don't do that,
Don't pull faces,
Don't tease the cat,
Don't be rude at school,
Who do they think I am?
Some kind of fool!

Don't put toffee in my coffee,
Don't throw jelly at the telly,
Don't put mustard in the custard
Who do they think I am some kind of fool!

One day they'll say
Don't put your toes up my nose
Don't pour gravy on the baby
Who do they think I am some kind of fool.

Zoe Watson (8)
Woolavington Village Primary School